Other books from Dale A. Darling

available at www.riverforkpress.com

High Waters

The Blacker Compendium, with Bob Frandsen

*Fly Fishing Colorado's Big Thompson River
and other freestone streams*

Solution Books

Getting Started

Fish! Bugs! Flies!

Presentation 101

Full color Kindle versions, excluding
The Blacker Compendium, available at amazon.com

HIGH WATERS

COLORADO'S 2013 FLOOD

DALE A. DARLING

With Love,

Dale A. Darling

RIVER FORK PRESS

www.riverforkpress.com

HIGH WATERS
COLORADO'S 2013 FLOOD
By Dale A. Darling
Copyright © 2014 by Dale A. Darling

Book & Cover design by Dale A. Darling

RIVER FORK PRESS
PO Box 7314
Loveland, CO 80537 USA
www.riverforkpress.com

Printed in the United States of America

First printing June 2014
ISBN-978-0-9832835-7-7

Thanks be to God for all things

For Shan, Rachel, Brittany, Jessica, Aaron, Russ and Addison Rose with love

To Don, Blake and everyone who helps

ACKNOWLEDGMENTS

No book happens without the encouragement and assistance of many individuals. Anyone who knows me will understand that my first thanks is to God and His Son Jesus for all things.

Shan and I went through the flood, as we have in life for the past 36 years, together. She has been a beacon of love, hope, good humor and grace. Her comments and tireless reads, which have uncovered deep emotions and evoked many tears, and the details she illuminated made this possible.

Family members and friends helped. Jessica's smile always delights and encourages, as do Rachel, Aaron, Addy, Brittany and Russ. Russ's early reads and comments helped keep me going and put me straight. Mom, John, Marvin, Jacque, and Bill Pattison read and contributed useful comments that made the book better. Elliott's critiques, humor and scholarly insight pushed me to decide and make further edits that were tough to do, but very useful. If I accomplished half of what he said, the book is far clearer and more concise. In the final stage, Vivian showed me a better way concerning the book's interior design, as did Val with its cover.

Thanks everybody!

Since I wrote, set and designed the book, and took many of the pictures and edited all of them, the mistakes you'll no doubt still find are mine, as are my opinions and my comments on the flood, it's aftermath and how I find God in all things.

Dale, May 2014

CONTENTS

Cover Photos

Front: Dawn Thursday, September 12, 2013

Back: One month later on our first trip back to our home

With a friend on the Big Thompson River

INTRODUCTION

In this book, I've recorded my thoughts and observations of the Colorado Flood of September 2013 as my wife, Shan, and I experienced it from our home in the Big Thompson River canyon at Drake, and its aftermath as survivor refugees in Loveland, Colorado. Writing them, then making multiple edits, has illuminated and brought perspective to the shades of events that we witnessed, and how people - including Shan and I - responded to them. I hope the book will do so for you, dear reader.

The idea for a book began on September 12 while we were still on the mountain, isolated from everyone other than 22 neighbors, and continued as we were flown out by helicopters on the afternoon of September 14. I jotted notes or wrote chapters over the next 45 days or so as the stream of emotions, thoughts and vignettes came to me, and as events continued to occur, until I felt their clarity began to dim. This resulted in uneven writing due to my own unsettled thoughts and emotions, the disruptive nature of the experience, and the ensuing disruptive unsettledness that continues. In specific vignettes, which you'll recognize, I've retained the original writing to express that nature. The flood was powerful and elicited a variety of sudden, often surprising, reactions and created a unique set of circumstances. The disjointedness of the experience and its remnants continue: we, and many others, have questions but few answers.

During those 45-plus days, I sent mass emails to family and friends that recorded what was going on, and inserted several, as well as a few responses, into this missive. They tell the story as it unfolded. I included pictures with each e-mail, and have included many in the book.

The book and pictures are printed in black and white so I can have it printed in the US, to keep its price down, and to pollute less. Color photos are available at www.riverforkpress.com, or on the Kindle version available at amazon.com

Here is my journal concerning what's now being referred to as the 500-Year, or Historic 2013, Colorado Flood. I hope you enjoy reading it, that it brings perspective. Mostly, I hope you'll accept it as the report it's meant to be, and as the note of thanks I want it to be.

Thanks for reading.

Dale - May, 2014

Our small cabin home on a typical Colorado summer day

Jessica and Chloe in the yard at the cabin

The cabin was a gathering place
Family and friends July 2013 by the Colorado Blue Spruce

Geert - Keith in background - fish the river by the cabin
Monday, just before the rain started to fall

BEGINNINGS

On a very hot, humid day in August 1978, Shan and I got married in Cambridge, Ohio, in her hometown church. We set up a modest household in Akron, where we'd met and where she had one remaining semester at the University of Akron. That May, I'd finished a Masters program in music composition at The University of Akron, and while Shan fulfilled the student teaching requirement to complete her degree, I tried to figure out what was next. With thought and prayer, we determined a course of action, and in July 1979, Shan and I moved to Boulder, Colorado.

Our move came three years after the 1976 Big Thompson Flood. I vividly recall hearing reports of that deadly event, of being awestruck by it, but, even though my imagination flourished with images, having no real idea of what it would have been like to be there, let alone in it. As I'd listened to and read reports of the flood, I also remember sensing a kinship for the canyon that I didn't understand, and questioning the source of that perceived connection. It was mystical and felt odd, but I let it go. I'd never been to Colorado, let alone visited the Big Thompson River Canyon.

We bought a house and moved to Longmont in 1985, and in 1989, after the birth of our third daughter - Jessica was a month old, Brittany three-and-a-half, and Rachel past seven at the time - I completed a doctorate in music composition at The University of Colorado at Boulder (CU). In addition to a family, mortgage and the advanced degree, I'd also learned and embraced fly fishing. After deciding that the bureaucracy of the university and I would not coexist, we opened a fly fishing pro shop in Longmont in May 1991. In 1993 we opened a second store in Estes Park and I started fishing the Big Thompson River through its canyon, falling in love with the stream and its environs.

While working 90 hours a week, and after opening a third store in Westminster and moving the Longmont shop to a new location in the same week in 1996 - operating a small business is pretty consuming, as it turns out - Shan and I talked and dreamed about finding a getaway. I hoped it would be on a trout stream, but didn't think that was possible. However, in 2001 we found and bought a cabin in Drake, seventy paces from the Big Thompson River (the Big T; or T). The mortgage company insisted that the property was not in the flood plain, that we would not need flood insurance. We questioned that announcement, but trusted the experts. Two weeks after we closed on the humble but nicely located property, airplanes flew into the Twin Towers in New York City and our starting-to-thrive business stood still. It began going backwards when two years of drought and forest fires followed. Government and media hysterics did not encourage fly fishing or any other outdoor activity; tourism dipped and the business began to fade. We held on through 2005, closed the last shop in February 2006, lost our house in Longmont during the summer of 2007, and moved to the cabin that July. It became our home.

Little did we think that we'd experience a similar event to the one I'd empathized with in 1976.

T he Big Thompson Canyon is 25 miles long and drops 2,500 feet in elevation as it travels east from Olympus Dam at Estes Park to the Dam Store just east of the narrows. On July 31, 1976, 3,500 tourists populated canyon campgrounds, hotels, homes and so on. Three large storms met to form a massive thunderstorm that day near Estes Park. It started to rain that afternoon, and in about 4 hours, 12-1/2 inches of

When we'd drive the canyon road, which followed the river most of the way - the areas where the most damage was done this time were stretches rebuilt following the '76 flood to avoid future destruction (!) - we'd point out scars caused by the flood, debris left in its wake. I'm sure the recent flood, our flood, washed away old and created new scars of its own when old, buried debris was displaced before being replaced with new stuff that will be exposed after the next flood. Who knew floods could be so greedy?

This time, the water stayed in its bed through narrow canyon and other natural stretches, rising as high as was required to move onward and downward. After high water that came out of the natural riverbed receded, it returned to the original course. Through wider swaths, where mountain roots were farther separated and man had placed and channelized the streambed according to his lights to protect the road, the water ruined the contrived bed and went where it wanted to go. The new bed, created in response to the massive flow of water, showed where the river wanted to be - probably the same place it ended up after the '76 flood. But in response to that disaster and in an attempt to protect the road and other property, the riverbed had been moved for importunate convenience. Under duress, a river responds to the water and does river very well, you see. It'll do it next time, too. This time, the post-'76 contrived riverbed stretches were destroyed, as was the road, its bed, homes and so on, and the river once again went where it pleased.

Our flood, the 2013 Historic Flood, was different than the one in '76, but still involved a lot of water. This time, it started raining on Monday afternoon, September 9, 2013. By September 16, 2013, up to 17 inches of rain had fallen. (The area averages 20.7 inches a year.) This time, the rain was less concentrated than that which caused the '76

Big Thompson Canyon Flood. This time the storm sat over Colorado's Front Range from about central Denver north to about the Poudre River drainage, and from the Continental Divide east onto the plains. The heaviest rain fell from just south of Boulder to north of the Big Thompson. Massive flooding occurred in Boulder Creek, Left Hand Creek, The St. Vrain River, the Little Thompson, Big Thompson and North Fork of the Big Thompson rivers, and in Rist Canyon south of the Poudre River. (That area had been ravaged by the High Park Fire of 2012, and the lack of foliage caused flash flooding even though a stream does not transverse that area.) Colorado State University estimates that our flood was a 1-in-1,000 year event, which doubles the popular 500-Year Flood moniker.

The Colorado and Wyoming National Guard evacuated 3,700 people and 1,000 pets. Eight people died. Estimates say there was $2 billion in damage, compared to $140 million (in 2013 dollars) in the '76 flood. I don't have the damage splits on specific areas, but you see that this flood was much worse for property and governments. Today our system functions more out of materialism than it did during 1976 - in that presidential election I remember discussion of morality and liberty; in the 2012 election, the talk was about the economy and individual security, basically about how people can keep their stuff if they'll just give away more liberty. Oh well. This post-flood talk is all about property damage and the cost of repairs. Most people that I've met who lived in the canyon during the '76 flood talk about people who died, friends they lost, families who were torn apart, and so on.

I've tried to figure another method to compare the two floods. My focus is on the Big Thompson and the North Fork at Drake because that's what we saw.

Water that flows in a river is measured in cubic feet per second (cfs). A cubic foot of water has 7.48 gallons, so one cfs means that about 7-1/2 gallons of water flow past a given spot in one second. Water that is stored is measured in acre feet. An acre covered with one foot of water, called an acre foot of water, has 325,851 gallons of water. On average, one acre foot of water provides enough for a Colorado family of four or five for one year. (California uses 35 million acre feet of water per year, much of this comes from Colorado.)

Here are estimates based on information I've gathered. (Keep in mind that I'm a composer, author and fly fisher, not a mathematician, okay?) On July 31, 1976 at 9 p.m. 32,700 cfs flowed through Drake. At 9:10 p.m. this was joined by a surge of 8,700 cfs that flowed down the North Fork. The North Fork is a tributary that joins the Big Thompson at Drake. If this amount of water - 41,400 cfs - flowed for one hour, that means that 1,114,835,000 gallons, or about 3,400 acre feet, of water went through Drake. That's enough water to serve 3,400 families for one year.

The estimates I've read say that on Thursday September 12, 2013 the water peaked in Drake at about 19,000 cfs in the Big Thompson, and at 18,400 on the North Fork. What I'll tell you is this: by late Thursday afternoon there was a lot of water flowing through our area. The streams themselves were no longer recognizable: water filled the entire canyon width. I did the following math by assuming this peak flow lasted for ten hours. I actually think it lasted longer than that, but this offers perspective for comparing the two flood events the Big Thompson Canyon has hosted during the past thirty-seven years. If 37,400 cfs flowed for ten hours, 10,007,121,600 gallons rushed down the canyon. My calculations say that is 30,900 acre feet of water. That's a lot of water, folks.

I think 30,900 acre feet - enough water for over 125,000 people for one year - is just over 9 times 3,400 acre feet. This makes CSU's estimate that the 2013 flood was a 1-in-1,000 year event about right if the '76 flood was a 1-in-100 year event. In addition to the peak flow, I did a rough calculation of the water's rise from about 6 a.m., when I projected a flow of 6,000 cfs, and 4 p.m., when I assumed the flow was at 30,000 cfs, an average of 1,500 acre feet per hour, or an additional 15,000 acre feet during that ten hour period. This means somewhere in the neighborhood of 46,000 acre feet of water - 14,989,146,000 gallons - flowed through our neighborhood on September 12-13. Again, I think there was more than that.

When full, Lake Estes holds 3,000 acre feet of water; Boulder Reservoir, 13,270 acre feet. Carter Lake holds 108,900 usable acre feet of water, so slightly less than half of its volume went through Drake in twenty hours.

One more bit of perspective. The typical September flow in the Big Thompson is under 100 cfs; the North Fork flows at under 10 cfs during the same month. Annually, an average of 200,000 acre feet of water flow through the Big Thompson Canyon. (Much of this comes by diverting Colorado River water east through tunnels.) We had about 25 percent of it in less than a day.

Like I said, it was a lot of water.

T oday, two weeks and a few days after our helicopter rides off the mountain, the sun is bright and the sky is clear: in other words, it's a standard issue, but never taken for granted, October 1 in Colorado. (For the first few years that my brother Don lived out here after moving from Ohio in 1993, he'd say, *Damn, another sunny day!* Colorado boasts 300 such days a year, and I'm pretty sure the other 65 occur in Ohio where we were raised.)

It's 7:27 a.m. Snow that fell a few days ago adorns the high peaks I see to the west along the Continental Divide. The prairie rolls off to the horizon in the other directions. The area is very green for October 1; we've had a lot of rain in what has been an interesting year for weather out here. But that's not unusual: folks in Colorado say if you don't like the weather, stick around. It would be unusual if there were a usual this close to the Continental Divide, at this elevation; but the sunny days are usual, are expected by Colorado's residents. People mope when a third overcast day follows two previous ones. (People moped during the week of the flood. And after.)

An early May 2013 snow; within two days, it was gone

The winter of 2012-2013 was dry until it started snowing in late March 2013. The media weather and disaster prognosticators drooled, based on the light precipitation, over the impending doom of severe drought, while they recalled and showed pictures or footage of the destructive fires of the previous late spring and early summer. But their story changed when it continued snowing throughout April and into May. Lots of snow piled up in the northern and south into the central Colorado Rockies, but the southern part of the state remained dry. Now the media had the worst of both worlds to report: floods and forest fires should be expected, but oh! how grateful we should feel about the runoff that would fill drought depleted reservoirs. Ski resorts reopened for a weekend or two in May, and Colorado would reap the economic benefits of more ski days! I know that fly fishers like me, and farmers, breathed a sigh of relief for the blessing of water.

In late May when the flow of the Big Thompson had risen to modest runoff levels Shan and I set up, prepared and primed our pump. Most of the water from snow melt in Rocky Mountain National Park is diverted at Lake Estes through pipes and ditches that are part of the complex Northern Colorado Water Conservation District plumbing system, which moves water to and stores it in three storage reservoirs. Boulder Reservoir (13,270 acre feet), Carter Lake (112,230 acre feet), and Horsetooth Reservoir (156,735 acre feet), dot the northern Front Range foothills and plains. That water, owned by and delivered to municipalities and agricultural stake holders, is used primarily to water lawns, trees and crops that 19th century explorers said wouldn't grow in the arid, sandy soil they found. I guess we fooled them, huh?

W hen Shan and I moved to Colorado in July 1979, I knew I wanted to learn to fly fish. Of course my main focus, other than loving my new wife - we celebrated our first wedding anniversary less than a month after arriving in Boulder - was learning more about composing music and playing the piano while taking doctoral work and teaching at CU. Within short order, I started tying flies and fly fishing, which led to learning all sorts of other new things. Fly fishing refreshes, and is a pleasantly addictive affliction. It was a great foil to classes, teaching, composing and practicing.

As a fly fisher, I learned about Colorado water law, about how water is owned and can be used. (What I learned was a big surprise to me.) In Ohio, when it was wet you mowed grass two times a week, and when it was dry you mowed green grass and left the brown alone. Lawns were splotchy.

In Colorado, lawns and grass on municipality byways was always green because everyone watered it from late spring through early fall. The water came from streams and rivers, which were developed to deliver and store water exclusively for agriculture or human consumption. Fly fishers complained about resultant stream flow issues that compromised trout habitat - as well as riparian habitat that supports all sorts of other life. I wondered why green grass was more important than wildlife habitat. And what I learned was that all of the water was owned by municipalities, ditch companies, land owners and so on, including downstream states that also depended on Colorado snowpack and runoff. Colorado's water courts were very busy. Buying and selling water was big business, and in reality, few cared about trout and other wildlife habitat. I also learned that putting or leaving water in a stream for anything other than human, industrial or agricultural use was prohibited. If a ditch company owned 50 cfs of water, and 50 cfs flowed past their head gate, they could take all of it. (If they don't use it, they lose it.) Trout? Well, the river would only be dry for a few hours. (A friend once said that water ditch riders should have to hold their breath, or be put in a room without oxygen, for as long as the stream was dry. No one took him up on it, though the streams often remained very low or were dewatered.)

A share of water, property with its own deed, came with the cabin. Each year we got a bill for $100 so we could use it. The money paid to rent the water. In most cases, a share of water is one acre foot, but the actual amount of water we "owned" was never made clear. But its use was. We could water trees and grass on our lot. We weren't allowed to use water pumped from our fresh water well for anything other than household consumption. *And don't wash cars with either water source!* The toilet drained into a small holding tank; gray water from sinks, the dishwasher, shower and washing machine went to a leech field that was in the yard. (I always thought it was in the front, but when the flood washed it away, I noticed the pipe from the house went into the side area, instead.)

We used water conservatively. Shan and I love flowers, and she studied to understand which plants would grow at 6,200 feet in elevation, taking into account the short season and the fact that our place was surrounded by 8,500-foot-tall foothills and lots of trees that blocked the sun's light. (It has been different awaking to that bright orb's light and presence in the morning during these first two weeks out of the mountains. I just realized how strange it is to again hear a train horn, too.) When the flowers started to show any sign of wilt, we fired up the pump and watered to perk them up. As long as the prime held, that is. Often, we'd lose the prime and have to begin the hours-long process to get it back while the flowers and grass continued to wilt. Summer afternoon sun fried the side of the cabin that faced southwest, so the flowers on and along the deck got watered often.

While certain canyon neighbors put fertilizer on their lawn and watered frequently to grow lush, green grass, as so many are accustomed to doing along Colorado's Front Range, I adamantly opposed both because the Big T, for me, was more than an irrigation ditch that carried water to keep my stuff green.

The Big Thompson is a trout stream. It teems with life that requires enough clean, cold, oxygenated water to thrive. There was no way I wanted to compromise either quality or coolness by adding pollutants that do both, or removing too much of it. Along the stream, I often found myself having mental arguments with people who had bought property along the stream and then cut down bushes, willows and other growth so they could sit on their deck and watch the water gurgle past. Cutting streamside vegetation does several bad things to trout streams, including warming the water by allowing harmful rays of light to penetrate and heat rocks, taking away shade and cover for trout, birds and the insects both species eat, and compromising stream banks that are held in place by the vegetation. But people who own land do as they please, fertilizing to grow greener grass, and cutting away streamside vegetation before pulling out root systems so they won't grow back.

As I said, the Big Thompson River is a dandy trout stream that teems with life. Trout, the aquatic insects they eat, and other organisms, thrive in and around the stream's clean, cold water. Our flood was fast and furious, a speck on history's long time line. Yes, it's easy enough to get caught in the tyranny and immediacy of that speck, to feel loss and emptiness that seems only to have smelly brown mucky goo all around, to feel as though it's permanent. But I know such feelings are not true, must not be obeyed.

While wading and fly fishing the Big T, I admit to occasional quick thoughts that I was standing in a bed of destruction and death when I recalled the '76 flood. Such thoughts were usually replaced by a trout rising to an insect or my dry fly, or by some other sign of life, like an American Dipper, or Ouzel, diving into the water, then flapping its wings underwater to hold its position while waiting to intercept an aquatic insect or minnow with its beak. Observing nature while wading in a trout stream is delightful.

Colorado is a state populated by immigrants. Within a few months after we moved to Colorado, I began to realize that people who lived here were very friendly, but that this trait lacked depth because of what seemed to be a lack of commitment to others. It appeared that those who had the courage to make such a move, while expressing character, might also have been trying to escape, to build a new life that resulted in a thin but impenetrable veneer, a friendly aloofness. This was, and continues, to be difficult for me.

And many natives were put out with us because they didn't appreciate or approve of the influx of new people.

When we bought the cabin, I thought we might find a few kindred spirits up in the foothills. Of the 24 neighbors who were present during the flood, other than one child and three adults, I think everyone was born and at least partially raised in another state before moving to Colorado. Shan and I moved from Ohio to Boulder in July 1979; other neighbors had come from Illinois, New York, Connecticut, Kansas, Texas, Ohio, Iowa and so on. This created what could have been an interesting blend. When Shan and I went to the cabin we hosted cookouts. I shared flies, tried to visit with people, and so on. Sadly, we ended up realizing we were surrounded by run-away-and-hide sorts, or something like that, instead. These leave-me-alone types perhaps more honestly embraced the common code from the 1960s that said, *As long as I don't hurt anyone else I should be a allowed to do whatever I want to do,* which actually means, *I'll do as I please without regard of anyone else, just leave me alone!* At least that's how it played out for the most part in our neighborhood, and often with others who lived along the canyon; that's what I observed, anyway. At best, Shan and I experienced lukewarm, superficial friendliness with little-to-no warm depth.

Everyone has a belly button and an opinion, of course, and our neighborhood, in my opinion, had many diverse opinions about its neighbors, few of which resulted in closeness or warmth. My friend, the author John Gierach says something like this: the guy you're fishing with is the best person on the stream; everyone else is an asshole. But in our neighborhood, it seemed that everyone, more or less and depending on the day or the issue at hand, thought everybody else was an asshole. Or both. There were few partnerships.

Disagreements have two sides. And it's true that I tend to flip people's switches because of my questioning manner. Out of curiosity, I often ask the *Is that true?* question and folks who seem to take odd ownership of their statements, who ascribe emotional affection for them, take offense. The question must imply, after people jump over various and sundry irrational hurdles, that I'm calling them a liar. But *Is that true?* applies to a statement, not the speaker. Still, reasonable conversation should include differences so they are interesting. Alas, preconceived notions and assumptions about others weighed heavily on my neighbors, who at first clearly expressed them to me, but over time, spoke to me less or not at all, especially after we moved and lived full-time in the cabin. Shan worked and saw less of it; she also had less tolerance for these shenanigans when she did see them.

I observed a tremendous capacity for impertinent whininess that, along with persistent head-shaking and arm-waving, was often bitchily expressed. It seemed like there was an underlying glee for thinking up and spouting conspiracies, perhaps to shift blame or to endeavor to deal with individual fears and insecurities. During our frequent early cookouts and visits - many neighbors attended - invariably, petty bellyaching and name-calling started. Shan couldn't tolerate such behavior; it sickened both of us. We stopped group invites while continuing to host a few individual gatherings. Eventually, they ended, as well. And I wasn't aware of much other interaction within or between neighbors, other than the occasional wave - or scowl - and backhanded stabs, when a neighbor deigned to speak to me, from this person about that one. It was lonely.

When we bought the cabin, the entire neighborhood was addressed as 1600 Big Thompson Canyon Road, and each lot had a number - 1600B1, for example. The addresses befuddled delivery drivers until they figured out which specific house belonged to which specific name on a parcel. Our place, being the first at 1600 Big Thompson Canyon Road, became the first stop for drivers, whom I assisted as I was able. At some point in time - apparently, emergency personnel also had a hard time figuring out where they needed to go - Larimer County officials decided that every street along the canyon needed a name. Ballots were sent to residents for suggestions and votes to determine street names. After the streets were named each home received a number. Great!

The street-naming vote occurred while our primary residence remained in Longmont. One of our Drake neighbors mailed us a ballot, which included the note, *We think River Fork Road is a good name; please vote.* It was the only contact we received concerning the issue, and I made the assumption that it meant others in the neighborhood, as well as the one who sent us the ballot, agreed on the name. In a show of support, Shan and I voted yea on River Fork Road. We liked it just fine. Later, others, who apparently disapproved of that winning name, made out that the process was conspiratorial, saying their suggestion was better. (The road could have had seven names.) Any opportunity for a conspiracy or name-calling by a neighbor, other area dwellers, county, state, federal or Martian officials was embraced.

In fact, these sorts of things often mustered a few neighbors - who would happily stab temporary co-groupies in the back on other counts - into little cultist groups that tried to impose their wishes, or fears, on other neighbors because it was what they wanted, and to hell with the rest. The list of such events and collaborative crap is long, the topics sordid and diverse. By comparison, the road naming was as child's play, even though most of the nauseating arguments were childish.

I started thinking a more accurately descriptive name for our street would have been Insidious Court. But no one would listen, and I don't think the County was interested in the paper work required for such an amendment. I never submitted the change.

The flood brought us near in spite of all that.

FLOOD

Early Monday afternoon, September 9, 2013, while visiting friends and I fly fished Colorado's Big Thompson River near Drake, Colorado, it started to rain. Colorado is an arid state that averages 20 inches of moisture each year. It falls at odd times, either as rain or snow. September is usually a dry month, but 2013 had been odd with very little snowfall until late March, persistent heavy snowfall through early May, then extreme, dry conditions until very late June, when we started getting consistent, and sometimes heavy, afternoon rain showers and thunderstorms. Most of the time, rain is welcome in Colorado.

On that Monday, another special day of several in a row with Jeff from Austin, Texas, Geert from Belgium, and Keith from Littleton, Colorado, I was not disappointed by the onset of an early afternoon shower. Light September rain often causes little olive mayflies to emerge and trout to rise and feed freely. I hoped that my friends would hook a few trout on dry flies. (The fishing was great; the catching pretty good.) A few small insects did emerge, but the rain didn't stop. In fact, it got heavier and continued until Friday morning, September 13, after which there were sprinkles for several days. The sky stayed dark, laded with heavy gray clouds. It rained hard.

And by very early Thursday morning, September 12, 2013, before the sun rose, water was out of the riverbed and flowed down River Fork Road and across our lawn. The rain kept falling and the water kept rising all day. Before dawn that morning, the canyon road, State Highway 34, was closed due to high water; by mid-afternoon, the water spanned the width of the canyon at Drake - It's over 200 yards across; by late that night, long stretches of the road were washed out, and many homes, bridges, vehicles and other things washed away in the torrent of loud, powerful water. And it kept raining; the water continued to rise.

T he typically docile stream stayed in its bed. But this morning, water-rising day, its water roared and fled the bed. The water that stayed within the confines of the still defined streambed was like a locomotive powered by evil, its demons pulling with great power, yet pushed by a legion. At first, the water that moved down our street and across our yard mimed the once docile flowing stream water, gently gliding past. But this was as a veneer of water scouts probing new area, once dry, that soon would be saturated, consumed, then ruined beyond recognition. Within a few hours the pulling, pushing legion of demons released all of their terrible energy and the canyon was full, a roaring torrent of filthy stink, carrying the scent of horror and the residue of death through its relentless path of destruction.

Dawn Thursday: water rising and flowing in our yard

As the water rose: an immutable hope in the present - we kept putting things up higher, including Chloe, Jessica's Holland Lop bunny. The water's rising: we can hold this back; this is going to work! Sandbags, towels, carpet, etc. Shan: "I wanted to replace the carpet in this room anyway - I was giving up this room."

We took "sips" of ideas rather than drinking through a firehose - and the water continued to rise.

It was very interesting; while moving stuff, Shan told the water, "You can't go across this line!" The piano was beyond the line. Shan held that line, arms out, yelling, "Water, stop!"

As the carpet bubbled up, Shan gave it up, knew it was gone. Realized I was outside, and we had to get out NOW! As soon as I was inside, Shan let go and gave up the house to the water. She told me so as we held one another, cried in my arms, wept and grieved as the water continued to rise around our ankles.

Later, as we stood outside our ruined home, she said, "I yelled at the water to stop, because it was going to get the piano! It was a connection with you, it was such a part of you!" Tears, a rush of emotion, followed.

It was powerful.

Thursday, the-water-is-rising-day, became a blur. Very early, before the sunlight had invaded the canyon, Sarah called to tell us that Ed had, on his drive down the canyon, been turned back by a Larimer County Sheriff's officer. (We had not yet received any calls of warning or to evacuate.) Ed left by 5 a.m. most days, and drove the company's white Chevy pickup down the canyon on his way to work. Shan was up preparing to go to work, too, so I think Sarah's call came before 6 a.m. It was raining and calm, as it had been since early Monday afternoon.

Shan called her boss, Rick, to say she wasn't going to be able to drive to work, that the road was closed. He asked if she'd be able to get there for the afternoon, said they had full columns of appointments scheduled, and it would be tough without her. Shan said she couldn't say, told him it was raining hard, that if it stopped and the road opened, which we expected, she'd let him know, and be there. He requested a call by noon. We thought she'd miss just the half-day of work.

By then, the bleak morning sunlight illuminated what we heard: heavy rainfall. We also saw the brown and turbid water that rushed through the streambed. The roar of sound was remarkable, like nothing we'd heard from the river before. And while we usually did hear the water, which was part of the charm of living here, we'd never seen the water flowing in the streambed from the cabin. We'd also never had water flowing down River Fork Road and through our yard. But there it was; it really caught our attention!

The water reflected a thin sheen of glare in the slowly increasing light, which continued to fight its way through the cloud cover. The raindrops, which made no impression on the water, obviously added to its flow. It kept rising.

"Ed is outside," said Shan, as I concurrently asked, "I wonder if the bridge will hold?" Looking out different windows, our minds were focused in different areas.

The bridge, via River Fork Road, connects our neighborhood, including the Chapel and CDOT, to Highway 34 near the Post Office, Drake Campground and Stage Stop Inn at the heart of Drake. We all knew the sturdy bridge was built to accommodate heavy trucks and other CDOT traffic.

Thinking ahead I said, "Shan, get the keys to the Subaru. We need to take the cars across the bridge."

I put on my hiking boots, and Shan her Crocs, retrieved my key to the Altima; we walked out the door for the first time that day. The light was dim. The rain fell. The water rose.

"Hey Ed," I yelled over the roar of the water, "you better drive a car across the river."

Dallas and Maggie were out, too. Dallas was thinking about disconnecting his pump at the river, and they argued. Maggie looked nervous. I could tell that Shan also wanted to plead with him to leave the pump. Many people killed in the 1976 flood were washed away by a wall of water while attempting to retrieve their pumps, and both women knew it.

"Dallas!" I yelled, "move a car across the river." We had to yell to be heard over the roaring water.

Shan and I started our cars, drove across the river, then parked between 34 and the river. Soon, Ed, and then Dallas, drove a vehicle across. We left my truck; Ed and Sarah left their other vehicles and Ed's work truck on our side; Dallas kept his old Willys, VW Bug and Ford Pickup at his place, but moved the bug and pickup to what I suppose he thought would be safe spots. None of us thought the water would keep rising.

But it was higher, and kept rising. When we walked back across the bridge to the neighborhood, the bridge vibrated.

"Do you think it will hold?" Shan asked.

"I guess we'll see," I answered.

We were alarmed.

Back at the cabin, I walked through a sheen of water to my pickup, the first new vehicle we'd ever bought. My hip waders were still on the floor of the 1994 maroon Chevy half ton, left there after the rainy day of fishing I'd done with Geert and Chuck on Tuesday. As I pulled out the hippers, I took note of my vest, and three fly rods and reels that were on the front seat. Two of the rods, both bamboo, were my favorites. I thought about taking the gear with me, but the

*The view looking downstream from our bridge
after we moved the cars*

present reality of the roaring stream, where, two days earlier, my friends and I had fished and caught wild trout on dry flies, distracted my attention. And, since my mind said there was no way that the water would get high enough to damage it, I thought *I'll get it later*.

Shan was inside when I arrived. I sat the waders on a piece of rug to keep them from sullying the carpet, and took off the hiking boots, which would no longer keep my feet dry. It was still raining. The water was still rising. Shan's shoes, and then my boots, just fit near Max's water dish. We tossed our already soggy rain jackets over the footwear, because we didn't want to get the carpet wet.

Max was nervous, paced the floor and stayed where we were. We'd tied him outside earlier so he could go potty on the grass before we fed him breakfast; our normal morning ritual. It was the last drop of urine that grass would absorb, the last meal that Max would eat in the cabin. But we didn't know that then. Chloe, I call her Miss Bunny, looked calm in her cage on the floor near the piano. Rabbits aren't very aware, let alone dramatic.

I turned on the computer, and got online to see if any useful weather info was available. Meanwhile, the phone started to ring. Concerned family members and friends, who were watching or listening to the news, wondered how we were. They knew more than we did, other than what we could see outside our doors and windows. It kept raining. The water, and the sun, continued to rise.

"We're fine," I said to each caller. "It's raining hard and the water is rising fast."

In each case, I said we'd let them know what we knew, but asked them to stop calling because we wanted to keep the phone line free. A few seemed put out by this; but most understood. Soon, we got a Larimer County Sheriff auto call. It warned us that at seven-o-something or another that morning, the spillway at Olympus Dam (it creates Lake Estes ten miles west of Drake) was opened to avoid a breech. We should expect a surge of water, it said, but promised the riverbed would hold the water within the confines of its banks.

Right. The reason water was now flowing down our street, and through our yard after rushing through the fence between our drive and the Chapel's lot and under and around my truck, was because the water had already left the stream's bed about 250 yards above the cabin. The call offered misinformation and wasn't very comforting. The phone kept ringing; we answered, talked, and continued to ask folks to wait.

When we looked outside, our eyes focused on the bridge, the truck's tires and the side deck: we used each thing to track the water's level. Eventually, the height of the waves in the streambed, then the standing waves in our yard, also captured our imaginations, and focused our attention. By 7:30 or so I didn't feel comfortable wading through the yard to cross the street. There was no way to cross the bridge, and soon no way to get to it. The water was too high. It lapped at the deck, was about a third up the truck's tires and splashed over after it breached the bridge.

"Shan," I said between phone calls, "fill every vessel we have with fresh water while the power is on and the pump will work. I'm going to take and send pictures, then write an e-mail for family and friends so they can see what is going on." That was also the first time I thought about making this book.

I took pictures with the Canon waterproof camera that my friend Gary Thim had gifted me for my 60th birthday the year before. Once transferred to the computer, I edited the pictures for size, then attached them to an e-mail I composed. This is the e-mail, which was sent at 9:32 a.m., September 12, 2013.

Hi,

Thank for your emails and calls. Right now it would be best to not call us as we're in the midst of heavy rain and flooding. We moved 2 cars across the bridge, and so far the bridge has not washed away.

The river is over the banks just upstream of the cabin and water is flowing across the lawn, the deck and down the driveway. So far, the level seems to have peaked and has fallen an inch or so - I'm watching my truck tires. I built a makeshift diversion by our side door, and that is keeping water out of that part of the cabin. Some has come in

Looking out the front sliding door just before sending email

the back door, and the garage is flooded. Some stuff has washed out of our hillbilly carport, and a few of the lighter flower pots are gone. I suspect the newly planted flowers will be gone. Oh well.

Route 34 is closed above and below Drake. Some bridges have washed away on County Road 43 along the North Fork, so it's closed as well.

Not much more to say. Again, after watching the water levels on the truck tires, I see that the water has dropped 2-3 inches.

The pictures will tell the story.

I hope you are all well. There will be a good deal of damage around here, and the rain is supposed to continue.

In the past 10 minutes, the water has dropped another 3-4 inches, and is no longer coming over the deck!

Love,

Dale

PS: poor Max is very nervous, has been pacing all of the time!

W hen I observed and wrote that the water had dropped, I felt relief. My belief that we'd seen the highest water would come true! As it turns out, the higher water was from the surge created when another gate at the dam was opened, and the drop in its level was a ruse that fooled us into temporary relief.

Shan's bother, Bill, who was on vacation in Peru, was the first to answer; his e-mail was followed by others. I answered each about like this:

We just got an evacuation order from the Sheriff's office; not sure what we'll do. Supposed to keep raining through tomorrow - lots of water right now.

Electric is still on; pump working. I guess we'll see what we can do.

Thanks.

A dear friend wrote; asked if we could get out.

I answered:

I'm really not sure we can get across the bridge, but don't worry.

There are 4 homes above us that are plenty high and 2 folks have said we can go there.

Our daughter Brittany, who lives with her husband Russ in Kansas City, Missouri, became one of several e-mail brokers during the next few days. (Of course we didn't know this until later.) Britt sent us an e-mail while the power was still on:

Hey Dad,

Thanks for the photos and update. I love you guys. How are things going now? We're praying for a smooth adventure with minimal damage. Love you! I'm sure you're busy, but if you get a chance I'd love to hear how things are going.

Love you, I'm glad you're my dad.

Love, Britt

At that point we knew it was impossible to cross the bridge due to the volume of water that was racing through the yard, as though yard and road were now part of the river's system. But there didn't seem any reason to worry family and friends while we still thought the water would crest and begin to drop.

Within a few minutes of my e-mail, the phone rang over and again. There was another stern warning call from the Auto-Sheriff, but there was nothing we could do. It kept raining. The water kept rising. Max continued to pace, ever dog-alert, hearing and sensing impending changes. For the moment, Shan and I were alert, too, but we had human calmness based on what turned out to be illogical reasoning that was based on irrational speculation. We weren't worried. It was September. It never rained this much during September in Colorado; there was no way it would continue.

Before 9 a.m., Shan took Max, and the camera, for a hike. They walked up Sly Fox Road, their usual point of departure, then cut down the back way to a gully; it was rushing with water. Along the way, she discovered that the entrance to her favorite riverside hiking trail was gone. "It was like it was never there," she said, "it was just gone! The rising water had taken away the whole piece of the neighbor's property and their big shed, also. While I watched, I could see the water still in the riverbed eating away the ground under the Highway 34, tugging against the guardrail while pieces of blacktop broke off and were swept away by the water's force. What an adventure of discovery!"

When she explained it and we looked at the pictures she'd taken, Shan said, "It was obvious that the water had been very high. The road in front of Gib's was rutted from 1 to 2 feet deep, and there was lots of debris, including big tree limbs, deposited on the grass. But the water had receded."

Debris from the surge; note water undermining the road

Obviously, the surge of water the first Auto-Sheriff call had announced had come and gone, had breached the streambed above Drake, too.

After her return we continued to speculate about the rain and rising water, maintaining our thought that it had to stop.

It surely would stop, right? Our position changed when, after walking to the back of the cabin, Shan screamed, "Dale, the water's coming in the house!"

She was in the back bedroom, until just recently Jessica's room. I went back and found her with towels, which she was forcing into the door's sill. "Grab more towels!" she ordered. I obeyed.

At first, Shan was selective about which towels were acceptable for this job. You know: use the old stuff. That selectivity didn't last very long. When the water stopped seeping and began pouring into the room, the less acceptable became more useful. Soon, nearly every towel, blanket and other absorbent material we owned was thrust into service. Soon, everything was soaked. The carpet in the hall started to bubble up. *Darn!*

Later, Shan told me that, at first, she'd decided to sacrifice that room's floor covering to the water, but wanted to save the rest of the house's flooring. At the time, her mind was still focused on wet floors. She hated the 25-year-old, 1970s gold shag carpet that came with the place. After we bought it in 2001, we replaced the rest of the ugly carpet and other flooring, but she bemoaned the original gold stuff that remained in that room. When Jess lived in the room, the carpet was usually covered with piles of Jess' stuff, Max's bed and Max. But with Jess' move - her stuff now covered the floor in her own apartment - the despicable gold carpet was back in sight, back in mind. Max didn't care. For Shan, this sacrifice was easy to make. A little water; oops, carpet's shot; replace it; spruce up that part of the house.

Outside, the still-rising water had now breached the deck, which was 6 to 8 inches higher than the adjacent yard, and pushed against the sliding door. Shan and I left the back room, its doomed carpet and our soaked towels, and waded out to our hillbilly carport. After observing rising water and wet stuff, we lifted the lawn mower out of the water - it hadn't yet reached the engine - and put it and a few other items onto the high surface of the workbench. I thought about moving the pump - ours is at the end of the driveway and pulls rather than pushes river water - but dropped the idea based on my inventory of the rising, rushing water and its impending invasion of the cabin. The pump was heavy; it would stay put.

"Let's take the sandbags and pile them by the door," Shan said.

The sandbags were in the wheelbarrow, which conveniently had a flat tire. No water was in the barrow because it was under the carport's flat roof, but water was flowing through, was, by that time, over our ankles. I wore hip waders, Shan a pair of pink Crocs. Her jeans were rolled up to her knees. Water was moving fast through the red slatted fence that separated the Chapel's parking lot from our driveway, before flowing under or around the truck. The Chapel building caused fast water to move away from the carport, but the water that backed within it created a deepening eddy. Shan and I talked a little - we had to yell to hear one another - while we stood, looking at the heavy sandbags, the wheelbarrow's flat tire. And then Shan walked closer to the garage door and towards her potting items - some of which were floating in little circles on the rising eddy. And then I saw what she was after! Our little, old, red, Radio Flyer wagon, her favorite conveyance of gardening goodies, was under water, but held its position, ready to haul her soils, shovels and so on to the flower bed that needed attention. Shan, who loved her little red wagon, pulled it over to the sandbags, and we put them into the trusty little vehicle. We pulled the wagon and its final burden through the water to the deck and creatively arranged the sandbags along the length of the glass door. The water merrily took the path of least resistance away from and around the sandbags.

We used the truck tires and deck as reference points to gauge the water. Here, the water is up to the deck

Yeah! We smiled, then shared a high five, certain that we'd saved the cabin from further damage.

Shan and I went back inside. It kept raining. The water kept rising. The phone rang. Max paced. Bunny was calm.

I laid on the couch to rest my back, a common habit since surgery in 1985. I was 33 then, fifteen years after the car wreck that hurt it. When the surgeon reported that he didn't want to alarm me, but, *You have the back of an 85-year-old man*, I had been alarmed. Now, at 61, I loosely did the math, but had no idea if any other 111-year-old back felt like this or not. (Wasn't Bilbo celebrating his eleventy-first birthday when he fled the Shire for Rivendell? I wondered how his back felt? Of course I'm six-four, and the Hobbit was about four-seven.)

Shan came from observing the back room, looked at the glass door, and said, "The water is coming over the sandbags!" The back room gone, she wasn't ready to sacrifice the front of the house; she liked that carpet.

I got up, put on the waders, donned the now very soggy rain jacket and my favorite hat, Sweetgrass Rods, and walked out the front sliding door. The cabin was breaking the water, which was now over halfway up the tires on the truck and rising, and was flowing in rivulets while occasionally surging over the bridge.

A folding table, and old door and a few sheets of plywood remained in the carport. The red, slat fence, which separated the Chapel parking lot and our driveway, was buckled and leaned against the truck. With each view of these sorts of things, I thought *I'll be able to fix that*, or *I know someone who would help repair this*. The water would begin dropping soon. The rain must have stopped at higher elevations, will soon stop falling here. And so on.

I moved the large, flat materials to the deck and made deflectors that moved water away from the glass door. Care was required because the force of the water against the wide, flat objects pushed hard. I kept the thin portion of each parallel in the current as I moved them into position, then jury-rigged heavy items along their length in an attempt to keep them in place so they'd deflect the water away from the door. After doing what I could do, I waded across the deck to the front sliding door. Waders, shoes and rain jackets were there, now; access to the cabin through the back and side glass doors was no longer possible due to high, fast-moving water and the works I'd constructed to keep it out.

"Maybe we should be sure our most important papers won't get wet," said Shan.

"You know where they are," I answered. "Let me know if you need a hand collecting them. I've got to lie down and rest my back."

"Do you want some Advil?" Shan asked. She knows that I avoid taking drugs, after taking too much ibuprofen, in my opinion, for too many years before and after back surgery. Since my back hurt as much after the meds wore off as it had before I took them, I decided to live with the pain in deference to the long-term health of my liver and kidneys. Yes, I wondered about all of the other old guy stuff I'd acquired - the now-85 + 28-year-old back, Menier's disease and cataracts at age 40, and so on, wondered how long I was going to last. Who knows? Does anything we do actually lengthen our days? I try to do the right thing at the right time, other than when my smart ass switch is flipped, or when a bout of depression kicks in, that is.

Shan, my ever thoughtful, loving wife, brought, and I took, four Advil.

After returning with the report that important papers were safe, Shan announced that the water was now coming in the glass door. It wasn't a calm announcement, though. For the first time, the sound of alarm was in her voice. By now the phone had stopped ringing because the electricity was out; there would be no more emails. We were cut off from the world outside our small Drake neighborhood. Max continued to pace. The rain fell. The water rose.

We could see that massive amounts of debris in the form of brush, trees and bits of wood and metal had pushed against the bridge, which now forced water to flow around and over both approaches to it. One end of the Chapel's propane tank had come free and now poked through the broken red slat fence. It pushed harder against my truck due to the water's pressure and the other debris that was captured by and pushed against the fence. Ed's truck, which he'd parked adjacent to the propane tank and parallel to the fence, shifted positions as the water expressed its power. Its power was significant.

My works near the side door moved, yielding to the persistent force of the water. After once again donning my go-out-in-the-rain gear and wading out the front door, I looked again at my water-level indicators: water flowed around the bridge and over the pavement leading to and from it, rushed through the slats of the fence, under my truck, through the yard, over the deck and around Gib's stable and other horse buildings.

I thought, *The hay will be ruined,* not, at that point, thinking, *Heck, that hay will be gone in a little while.*

I also noticed a pleasant earthy, peat moss scent that carried a waft of pine. After a few delicious sniffs, however, I realized the scent had a minor invasion of raw sewage odors, a stink that soon permeated, then replaced the scent of pine: it was a portent of what would come. For the time being, the lilac bushes, Shan's flower bed and our grass held in spite of the olfactory data indicating that this was not the case upstream, that massive amounts of soil were being carried away in the muddy water. But surely the water was as high as it would get. Surely the grass, trees, flowers and so on would keep our dirt where it was.

Water on the deck in front of the cabin was deep but slow, like an eddy below a large rock in the stream where trout hold. (I like casting bushy dry flies to these spots!) But the water rushed over the other sections of deck, along the side of the cabin, and was now nearly knee deep.

While the deflectors continued to hold, the water snuck behind them, finding and filling every available space within its depth. I glanced at the truck tires: water now flowed over the axle, a few inches higher than the hub, about eight inches higher than my earlier optimistic e-mail had reported. And it kept raining. Shan's potted flowers - pots and all - were gone, according to size. The smallest departed first. I saw a large pot with a hosta plant float past the deck and thought of grabbing it, but considering the depth and speed of the water flowing on the deck, then adding 6 to 8 inches of depth and the appropriate pressure, and knowing that water was seeping through the glass door into the cabin, gave perspective to that drifting pot of flowers. I let it go, then waded back to the carport for another sheet of plywood, wagging my head at that meager loss, still optimistic about saving other stuff and the cabin. Neither Shan nor I took any bodily risks to try to save stuff.

I'd put a folding table, 5-feet long and 30-inches wide, against the side of the cabin, wedging it at an angle to the deck. It held, but the connection to the cabin was loose and water leaked past, flowed along the wall, past the next plywood deflector, over the sandbags and into the house. I made adjustments such as I could. While I watched the water push items off the deck as it rose and rushed around my minor works and thought about what else might work, I had the first sneaking suspicion that perhaps the water would not abate. That and every other thought ceased when I heard Shan scream, "Dale, get in here! We've got to get out!"

Sometimes, it is difficult to determine whether what you're doing now has purpose or not. (A good reason to do the right thing when you can do it.) I took a look at my works, realized that in spite of my optimism and purposeful attempt to protect our home, there was no hope that the works would hold. This was clearer when the Chapel's propane tank broke through our red slat fence, floated through our yard, and spewed gas into the air like a little tug boat blowing its steam whistle, wondering if it could. Our tank stayed put, but it was temporary courage on its part. Ed's truck was still there, on the upstream side of where the Chapel tank had been, but the force of the water had turned the big Chevy, had pushed it into the hole in the fence the propane tank had created when it fled. Water flowed around Sarah's SUV before pressing against the front tires of Ed's new, black Camaro, and then rushing down the road. Wood that Ed had split and stacked for winter fires in their massive stone fireplace, and yet-to-be-split logs, bobbed in the eddy downcurrent from their house.

I took it all in at a glance, pondered my sure-to-fail works, then bowed my head, sighed and waded across the deck to the front glass door. Patio furniture was pushed tight against the deck's rail. Shan's newly sewn cushions, like

Ed's logs, bobbed on the water around the furniture they were made to adorn before the current caught, then carried them over the rail and away. The furniture and deck would follow as soon as everything was properly prepared for it to go. Like so much other debris, ours too created in-the-water sails that multiplied the water's force, increased the damage.

When I opened the front door and walked in, I left the waders on, breaking a cabin rule: no waders to be worn indoors! (It was just as well that Shan didn't know about the times the rule had been broken by angling friends and I, but since all of that is now moot, I'll tell it here, but don't tell her.) Shan was in the bedroom, moving particular, meaningful items off of the floor, out of the closets and so on before placing them on our bed. She left all of our clothes hanging, still optimistic or unable - unwilling? - to imagine how high the water would get.

All of my girls at the cabin
Addy never drove the Camaro!

The items on the bed included her wedding gown - she asked if that mattered any more. I said, *We have one more daughter who wants to be a bride* - all of the baby blankets we'd used to warm our growing girls, two of which have been brides and are now wives, and so on. She found a few boxes of pictures, later, realized others were ruined - we miss them - and I piled my bamboo fly rods and two shotguns on the bed, too. All of that stuff was added to the drawer of important papers, Shan's work shoes and uniforms, and the other things deemed to be meaningful. I picked up the framed photo of Rachel standing by the red Camaro convertible, which Jessica drove into the river a few years earlier. (!) Rachel always said to me, "Daddy, I look better in the Camaro than you!" I always answered, "True! But it's daddy's toy, not Rachel's toy." I tossed the picture on the bed, too. Memories flooded my mind. All four of the girls enjoyed driving the car, and they all did look better in it than their husband and old man. Oh well, girls ganging up on daddy as they will and all, four-to-one was the usual vote.

We put a few clothes into small canvas bags. Shan grabbed the clutch of toiletries she kept ready for doing pre-work beautification, our toothbrushes and toothpaste, a few rolls of toilet paper and other odds and ends that, at the time, made sense. The dryer gurgled in the bathroom, which indicated that the crawl space was full of water; this brought another snarl of discontent. Bunny and her cage went on the couch. I grabbed a bag of Max's food. We donned the soggy rain jackets, hefted the bags and other stuff, looked at the rain falling outside and the water rising inside, looked at the piles of items Shan had stacked on another couch - my boxes of compositions, scores and so on - and walked out the front door of our home for the last time.

TO THE HIGH GROUNDS

Seven occupied households were in the flood's path. Nine of the twenty-four neighbors were safe in their four homes on the high grounds of Sly Fox Road, while the other fifteen from the low grounds were out of the safe and separate confines of their own homes. Of the four on the high grounds, three were adult couples without children, but all with pets - one had a dog, but two had cats! - and the other, Jason and Joy and their sons Gabe, 14, and Caleb, 5, had dogs.

Of the seven households on the low grounds, now in the flood plain as it turned out, only one had a child at home. One household was made up of a single woman and her dog. Four of the other five couples, save the one, had pets; six of seven had dogs, and one couple had a cat. Yes, on the low grounds there was one cat-controlled home. And only half of that household, the bride, liked the cat. Oh, and Shan and I had Jess' bunny, Chloe, who is cute, her only redeeming virtue, which is pretty good for a rabbit, all things being equal. Everyone in the neighborhood had a lifetime collection of stuff, and had made a home on River Fork Road in Drake, Colorado, along the banks of the Big Thompson River. Several other seasonally visited houses in the neighborhood were empty. Only permanent residents populated the area on this mid-week September day. The flood forced all of us into four homes and a camper along Sly Fox Road, where we were stranded for the duration.

I think the neighborhood, called the Haydn Subdivision, was developed in the 1950s, but it's possible that a few of the farthest upstream places were built earlier than that. One house was built in the mid-2000s, and another was built in 1977 on the site of a place that was washed away by the '76 flood. Our place had an addition constructed following that flood, and another neighbor built a garage on his property in the mid-2000s. One of the four high-ground homes had undergone beautiful remodeling, two of the others were prebuilt and hauled up the hill and assembled before becoming homes, and the fourth, an A frame, has been made into a delightful home. Just beyond the A frame, a camper on a truck perched above the Sly Fox extension, a picnic table and fire pit nearby. One of our two elderly couples resided there during the flood. An abandoned set of structures on the high grounds provided the only pit outhouse, which came into use when water was not available to flush toilets; meanwhile, millions of gallons of water carried raw sewage past the neighborhood and down the mountain. Consider the irony.

Sly Fox, a dirt road that rises quickly behind our cabin, gives access to the four high-ground homes, the abandoned property, and the truck camper. Gib, the neighborhood cowboy, occasionally rode his horse up the hill, while other neighbors, such as Shan, used it as the start of hikes into the lands above. When Max had one of his occasional I-need-to-be-a-bad-dog attacks that aligned with momentary freedom, he raced out of our yard and ran up Sly Fox, making sniffing stops at each of the upper three homes, before his foray was ended by capture or by a continuation of his walk back downhill to the river. He usually took a swim. But for the most part, Sly Fox was the high-ground neighbors' path to River Fork Road on their way to or from Highway 34.

And as divided as the neighborhood was - at one point, one of the flood plain residents badgered two of the high-ground households about sand that washed off the side of the mountain during rainstorms before flowing through the CDOT property and then along River Fork Road, depositing the sediment on the verge of his yard; one high-ground neighbor tried to sell their house as a result - Sly Fox did draw the four high-ground households together when the road needed repaired. Heavy rain, in addition to washing the sediment off the sides of the foothill, also cut one or two deep, then deeper troughs through or along the edge of the sneaky street, dumping the debris near the bottom of another driveway and causing havoc to axles, shocks, tires and nerves. More than once, the four families agreed to buy, have delivered, and spread truckloads of road base. It worked; the road was repaired! And it was cool to see their cooperation.

The steepness of Sly Fox, especially when combined with snow and ice, required that each of the upper three families drive 4-wheel, or all-wheel, drive vehicles. (The lower couple had 2-wheel drive cars, and when it was real bad, parked the cars at the bottom of their driveway.) When Jason and Joy first rented their place, before purchasing it, they had one 2-wheel drive vehicle, and when any snow fell, were forced to park at the bottom of the hill - sometimes, they used our driveway - and then walk to their place. It was quite a haul in the cold, especially with groceries, schoolbooks and their at-the-time infant son. When we saw them and Shan was around, we'd drive them up in her Subaru Forester. Eventually, they bought a Forester of their own, but before that purchase I never heard them complain.

I don't actually know who constructed or owned Sly Fox, but the neighbors took ownership and care of it, including, now and then, chasing off curious campers who ventured up the street for a look - there are two campgrounds across 34 in Drake - or, when whatever it was in the water increased local vitriol, now and again chasing off hiking neighbors from the low ground. In other words, they took some ownership; some responsibility. One posted a No Trespassing sign.

But when the water started to rise on September 12, 2013, we got calls from two of the four households telling us we were welcome to escape to their places. When we had to get out of the cabin, we spent Thursday and Friday night at one of the high ground-homes, ate one meal at one of the other homes on Friday, and were asked and permitted to put a few rescued items into a shed at yet another place. These were the only invites we'd ever had from any of the four, but we'd only owned the cabin since 2001. (Only one of the flood-plain people had ever asked us to visit their house.)

On the first day out, Friday the thirteenth(!), all of the neighbors helped one another, shared as they could and would - not always the same thing - thought about what might come next, consoled and tried to comfort one another, prepared for evacuation and behaved like people who actually cared for one another. Thoughtful patience occasionally burst forth. There might have been a fit of compassion now and again. It was great! By Saturday morning, however, a few were ready to kill one another, clearly stating their intentions to do so, as in, *If that son of a bitch comes near me again, I'm going to kill him and throw him into the river*. On the evening before, the two had shared grilled hamburgers. Still, a flood that brings temporary civility also does odd things to one's nerves.

Go figure.

So which is it? I can't really say because I don't know. Apparently, abrupt trials - those labeled a disaster - result in bonding that within short order must feel more like bondage than loving human ties. Just recall the post-9-11 outpouring of what proved to be phony - or, at the least temporary - patriotism, the outpouring of promised prayers and hatred for and against fellow Americans and Middle Eastern terrorists, respectively, and how fast all but the hateful contempt evaporated. Note that what was left was fear, as well as further suspension of civility and the curbing of liberty as expressed, in one vociferous and clear way, by the Transportation Security Administration in our airports, where everyone is guilty until proven innocent. Appalling.

In our neighborhood, the mien of civility and common good lasted for about one day, even though a fair number avoided others to feel safe or to avoid potential grief, which might be the same thing. Self-protection. Yes, there were fits of compassion, expressed by people who assisted and even carried their neighbors from the flood-plain to the high grounds, who figured out how to get electricity to operate an oxygen condenser, who gave up this or that for another, who carried a neighbor and their stuff or both back down the steep, muddy slope to the helicopter, who stayed longer than they might have in order to continue assisting others who also remained on the mountain. (Everyone was safely evacuated: great!)

Ed and Sarah fled from their home very early on Thursday, which had been an excellent call on their part. The water that breached the streambed upstream of our places rose fast as it flowed down the road that separated their house and our cabin. By the time they decided to leave their house, it was very difficult for Sarah to wade through the rising, rushing water. Ed had to carry Casper, their old dog, while Lucy, the young German Shepherd, waded with Sarah. Ed grabbed his Navy bag, which he kept packed and ready for Reserves' activities, but Sarah only had the clothes on her back. Like the rest of us, they thought the water would stop rising sooner than later, that they'd be back home later that day.

I was glad that Ed had been turned back while driving to work on Thursday morning, because Sarah's call to us at about 5:30 a.m., when he returned, was our first warning of the rising water. I was also glad Ed was with us during the flood: he used his considerable common sense skill to help our neighbors.

In the early afternoon of September 12, Shan, Max and I walked to the house on the hill Ed and Sarah had fled to that morning. The owner's husband had been called to work very early Thursday morning. She met us with "Mi casa es su casa!" and "This feels like old hippie days." She held and drank from a glass of wine that was constantly refilled. I was cautious of her happy disposition, caution based on a persistent rudeness she and her husband had expressed to me. Even though I wished for better, I would not be disappointed.

For the time being - Ed hadn't spoken to me for almost three years - there was an uncomfortable calm, as two-and-a-half couples were near, but kept their distance, in the small, beautiful home. One of the owner's cats was gone, and the other one was miffed by the presence of intruder dogs Max,

Casper and Lucy. Fair enough for a cat. Until the missing cat returned - it was a relief for all of us to see him - the owner became less comfortable and more worried and morose, which was also fair enough. I think she wondered about her husband, and I know she loves her pets.

Still, the uncomfortable calm was enhanced as our mutual unrest rose with the flood of water. So it goes. Soon, the *Mi casa es su casa* became *This is my house*, and a to hell with the neighbors attitude became clear. Shan argued with this We all tried to keep our distance from one another, and I have to say that even though the attitude made me sad for everyone, I wasn't surprised. When we saw her at the rescue center at Timberline Church in Ft. Collins after we were evacuated, she ignored and avoided us. When, a month later on our first trip back, I saw her husband near their house, he refused to acknowledge our presence in the neighborhood; it was normal behavior. They'd also thrown a few items outside that we had to leave up there when we so hurriedly evacuated, and it was wet.

A few weeks after our evacuation, it was Ed who called to let us know that the road was open, that he'd been down, had retrieved his truck and so on. Two months after that, we met Ed and Sarah at the Coffee Tree after I called to tell them about the long-term recovery group.

M y fishing and Ed's work truck, both Chevy pickups with toppers, but full of different types of important stuff, had drifted downstream on Thursday. We saw them go past our high grounds perch, and commented in surprise because neither of us thought the water would come that high, let alone float, then destroy, our trucks.

As the trucks were pushed along, but before they went not so merrily down the stream, we heard a loud CRACK! A moment later, our entire, still-in-tact L-shaped deck came into view. It floated to my truck, at the time temporarily stalled in

Shan stands in a driveway near where Sly Fox and River Fork Roads join. My truck sits for a moment in our front yard before the deck hit it and encouraged its continued drift downstream

the front yard between the Colorado Blue Spruce and the end of our front driveway. When the deck struck the front of the truck - it was backing down the deluge, powered by it - the truck started to move again. The deck took its own course until the water pushed it against one of the remaining trees along our drive, and stayed there until it broke apart. The tree also held other items that packed onto the deck until the tree was uprooted. Everything then disappeared in the roaring maw of the hungry flood.

Within moments, our beautiful blue spruce followed the truck
down the river while Shan watched and wept

Shan stood near and watched, her arms outstretched with surprise, as our truck drifted past, helpless to do anything about it. I don't know if, at that moment, she thought about the fact that all of our Christmas decorations were in the back of the truck, but later the thought that all of Jess' decorations and bulbs, collected yearly from her childhood, were gone made us both sad, made Shan weep. When, a few moments after the truck drifted past, the 40-foot-tall Colorado blue spruce - the gem of our front yard - followed, Shan held her hands up and cried at the loss. The Hupps, from whom we bought the cabin in 2001, had planted the tree after the 1976 flood, and its well-developed, but shallow roots, could not withstand this onslaught of water.

The spruce and my truck both drifted on past and out of sight, but Ed's truck struck, then stuck to, a telephone pole, and stayed put for a few hours while the water, and debris it carried, did their work. After they undermined the pole, water pushed the truck, pole and the cluster of other once precious stuff on their way, no doubt wreaking further destruction farther along before being ground to bits. Pieces of wrenches, screwdrivers and other now unidentifiable things probably filled new crevices that moving water and boulders formed in the new streambed.

A week or so later, someone reported that old cars buried after the '76 flood were exhumed by the water of this one, but I don't know if the report was verified or not. It wouldn't be too big of a surprise, considering how much substrate was disturbed and moved by the water that caused the 500-Year Flood, which is what they started calling this one. You know, whoever they are.

Chloe does one thing well: cute. She does it very well, captured safe and sound, in her comfortable cage.

In early September, Jessica moved from the cabin into a Loveland apartment she found and could afford. (Mixed feelings at the time turn to great joy after the flood!) It is close enough to walk to her job at the Coffee Tree when she wants, and close to the high school where she works with all of the bands' percussion sections. Jess wasn't sure about the legality of having bunny in the new place, because the lease stipulated no pets. And she hadn't gotten around to asking if Miss Bunny would be permitted or not. I mean a rabbit is not a cat or dog, after all. So, we'd continued caring for Chloe at the cabin, which meant I fed and watered her, and every several days suggested to Jess that it was time to come up and clean the cage.

When, as the water continued rising, Shan and I decided to get out we got food and a few treats for Max, but put bunny

Jessica and Chloe

on the couch, still thinking that the water wouldn't rise any higher. Our evacuation was temporary; bunny would be fine in her cage on the couch. This prophetic thought was on the list of many that did not turn out to be accurate. We meant well, but that didn't mean anything. The water would do its bidding.

A while after we'd walked up the hill in response to our neighbor's call to *Come up here; you're welcome to stay*, Shan and Rodney decided to go back to the cabin to get the bunny; to see if there was anything else to save. As they waded through knee-deep water inside, Shan noticed the water outside was half-way up the height of the side sliding glass door! Shan turned to get a blanket to throw over bunny and her cage and Rodney shouted, "Shan! We have to get out now!"

She and Rodney grabbed the cage with Chloe, and they dashed, such as they could through knee-deep-rising water, through the living room. A blanket Shan had earlier put on the floor to absorb water caught her ankle and almost upended her on the way. "It was like a slimy mass of living seaweed wrapped itself around my legs!" she said.

A moment later, Shan, Rodney and Miss Bunny were out the front door, and up the hill.

Chloe stayed with Rodney and Lily. I never heard a report about whether their cat thought the rabbit does cute. On Friday, when the rain stopped and a bit of blue sky peeked through the clouds for the first time in days, Lily put bunny outside in the sun. She found carrots, celery and other greens for bunny to munch; we forgot bunny's food, and by now it was gone with, as we soon find out, so much else.

On up the hill, Jason and Joy, older brother Gabriel and 5-year-old Caleb, were a picture of helpful generosity. They opened their home to a neighbor and her dog, then to Chris, her son, her boyfriend and his father, who was visiting. I think Chris' crew also had four dogs, and Jason, Joy and the boys had two; the humble home became a human and canine menagerie.

On Thursday morning, while the phones still worked, Joy had called to tell us we were welcome to stay with them. "Do you have enough room?" I asked.

She explained the layout - this was before anyone from the flood plain other than Ed and Sarah had left their home - and added, "But our vault is about full. Jason just yesterday called Marlo to come empty it."

The full vault - up here, so close to the river, no one has a septic system, so black water, the stuff that comes out of a toilet, is stored in a concrete vault until it's full; then, we call Marlo's Johnston Sanitation to come and suck it out and haul it off - made for creative ablutions. Most folks hiked up the dirt path that is ostensibly an extension of Sly Fox where, I assume, they found a comfortable spot to pee or take a dump.

On Friday, Gib wanted to show me his projected helipad, but on the way up the hill he said, "We should wait. I think someone went ahead to go to the bathroom." Sure enough, a few minutes later, someone came down the hill. To me, the look said, *They know!* We traded pleasantries - such as can be traded during a raging flood, and under the circumstances - without mention of anyone shitting in the woods. The bears do that up there all the time, and it really wasn't a big deal. Everyone needs a daily crap.

Several other neighbors also decided where the first helicopter would land. Ed and a couple others removed debris from one potential landing zone - or LZ, as Chris' son called it. Everyone was beginning to think about helicopters and what they would mean by Friday. That morning, after the rain stopped falling, various types of helicopters flew overhead fulfilling various duties.

Our first priority was that Carolyn, Gib's wife, needed oxygen. Marge's husband had given Carolyn all of his - he wore a tough face, said he was doing fine, but we weren't sure how long he'd be able to hold out. And I think most of the neighbors hoped these two active but elderly couples would soon be taken off the mountain and reunited with family that lived in Ft. Collins. Fresh water was also running low. Ed's mention of additional sources of water, such as drawing water out of the hot water heaters that no longer had power to heat the water - an excellent idea - gave a little relief to the anxious prospect of running out of drinking water. By now, I don't think anyone was using water to flush toilets. We'd discovered an outhouse in the previously mentioned abandoned building, and told the neighbors where it was. That was a comfort.

During Thursday afternoon and again on Friday, neighbors make their rounds down Sly Fox to stand near the roaring torrent that has swept River Fork Road down the canyon. In fact, a section of what was River Fork Road is now the Big Thompson River's bed as it flows from above the CDOT buildings past Dallas and Maggie's place, and past the Chapel, before flowing through what was our front yard, across Sly Fox and through Ace's old pasture, now his grave. Ace was killed by a car on the road two summers ago. The spot where we held a memorial service and he was buried is, with all of his buildings, gone along with all of the top soil. Ace's bones will be ground to wet dust, as will so much else. Gib's new horse,

John, was across the street by the campground when the water started rising. Later, we hear that the horse climbed the hill and wandered and grazed up on Storm Mountain. A week later, Gib got up on the mountain via a 4-wheeler, then rode John out; Gib is 88-years old.

Thursday September 12, flood day, was full of continuing drama and various degrees of surprise and shock, of ongoing but unfounded hope that the water was as high as it was going to get, that it wouldn't get higher. People we saw projected varying degrees of fear, shock, hope, a sense of humor or of impending doom, and a variety of other dispositions. Many peered through glassed over eyes. Everyone was tired.

During the course of Friday, the often dysfunctional neighborhood had twenty-four souls behaving rationally, speaking to and helping one another, often without too much thought for self. Cooperation ruled. People were thinking of others, for the most part, even though a few emotionally self-centered folks kept their distance, were rarely seen, and sulked when they were.

Chris was in shock, which was fair enough, because she and her son, her boyfriend and his father, had just escaped her home on Thursday night. The way I heard it, they were trying to sleep, when everyone noticed that the house began to vibrate. Within moments of climbing out the back door onto the deck, which was built into the mountainside, the house was dislodged from its foundation and swept away in the rush of rising water. It was very dark and still pouring rain. I imagine there were screams of surprise and terror, and heard that Jason helped Chris, the men and the dogs up the muddy hill to Jason's house.

Sarah, like her friend Chris, was having a tough time on Friday after Ed came back to where we stayed with news that, *It's all gone; everything is gone.* (Ed and Sarah's house was completely gone.) Ed held a firm upper lip and busied himself with trying to figure out what he could do to help others, while Sarah, a stoic Yank from Connecticut who doesn't openly express her emotions, kept a smile on her face around others. Her eyes told a different story. (I was pleased when Ed called a few weeks later and told me that Sarah was going to get some counseling, but wondered about him when he said he was fine, *It's just stuff.* When I saw him later that week in the neighborhood, his eyes and mien said he felt pretty sad at the loss; fair enough. But I'm quite certain Ed will be fine, and hope what Sarah learns will help them both through the mourning process.)

Chris' car, truck, Scout, modest RV, and boyfriend's dad's truck with all of his work tools washed away with the house. On Friday morning, we saw the wreckages of the RV, car and one of the trucks along what had been River Fork Road. Something stopped them there for some reason, but not before the entire package - house and vehicles - had destroyed half of an adjacent neighbor's home.

Other than a hole made by a tree trunk in the side of the CDOT Quonset hut, the two CDOT buildings withstood the water, which ran adjacent to both. A gravel bar that formed near the front of the hut - all of the asphalt pavement was gone - would be the LZ that the chopper pilots chose. (Our prognosticators guessed wrong.) A narrow bridge was required to span the creek that flowed around the gravel bar, and a length of guard rail, handy at CDOT, served that purpose.

Dallas' VW Bug and Ford pickup were mostly where he left them, but both were smashed with and smothered by debris, pushed against his garage and a tree. The ancient Willy's jeep was gone along with his wagon. The back of his garage, primarily a beautiful wood shop that occasionally garaged Maggie's Toyota, was blown out, and I suspect most of the tools and other items had followed. (Dallas moved the Toyota across the river on Thursday, after Shan, Ed and I had moved vehicles over there.)

On the walk to and fro, people stop to check on Rodney and Lily - today, everyone is checking up on other neighbors - and they all see bunny. In spite of the circumstances, ever cute, humble Chloe brings a smile to every face I see when I visit, and smile, too. Miss Bunny has that effect on people. Much of the time, smiles are few up here, other than for those who do smile, who have smiled. Sour pusses remain sad and become sadder. Those in shock from loss are a different case altogether.

Friday morning, after having fled our home for the high grounds and a neighbor's couch, Shan and I awoke, walked down the hill and found the front of our house blown out, the inside full of water and wet mud, the Sauter grand piano and most everything else apparently ruined with sand, gravel, mud and water. Two neighbors' homes were completely gone; others were damaged; many vehicles were either gone or stacked in piles like so much scrap metal, along with other people's upstream belongings that were strewn or lodged against still standing trees or posts, or deposited on new gravel bars the flood created. The riverbed my friends and I had waded and fished a few days earlier was completely full of boulders, rocks, stones, gravel, sand and other debris the water had deposited.

On Friday, Shan and I tried to salvage a few items from our house, and that was all we got: a few things. Neighbors milled around on the high ground, or walked to the base of Sly Fox Road, to where it had once joined River Fork Road, but now ended in a raging torrent of brown, stinky water. Some people commiserated and shared; others wandered. Various degrees of shock were recorded on many faces. The three children - boys aged 5, 15 and 16 - found adventure and, like their parents and other adults, tried to make sense of what in the world was going on. Many were on tenterhooks because of the often menacing nature of neighborhood relationships. We were completely cut off, isolated. Cell phones don't work up here, the power was out before noon on Thursday, and the last analog phone that worked quit later that day when our huge, beautiful Colorado blue spruce followed my pickup downstream and took out the last phone line and the poles that held it.

On Friday, as she looked out over the water that roared through the low grounds, Joy, mother of two of the boys, said, "I could have done with the remaining seventy-three years of that hundred-year flood." I'm pretty sure the rest of us shared her sentiment.

Later on Friday, a few helicopters flew high over our neighborhood, either scanning the area to create rescue reports, or shooting video to splash over the airwaves all around the world. (Friends from Europe, South Africa and Australia told me they saw the reports, saw Drake on TV. Our kids told us they saw our cars.) For Shan, the helicopters brought hope. She said, "They are up there, watching and checking on us, responding: they know we're here."

By late Friday morning it stopped raining. But the water continued rising. The mountains were beautiful, with puffy white clouds nestled into the bowls and deep cuts wrought during bygone floods. Clouds higher in the sky, once dark and ominous, were a little lighter than they'd been that week, which lightened our hearts. It rained on and off that day, but the rain was spotty, lighter and less relentless than it had been for the previous four days. Water continued running off the mountainsides as gravity did its work, as the water obeyed its call.

Ed and I were out of the house as the sun rose that morning, and we took a look over the lovely mountains, then at the hideous roaring strength of water that continued flowing past where we stood. From that spot, neither of us could see our homes. We knew our trucks were gone, but I think we had a sense of hope for the vehicles we'd moved, and we knew they'd been moved again. Soon, Shan joined us. And within a short time, she and I walked down the drive to take a look at our place.

L: Thursday afternoon - while the side sliding glass held, the water raced past. R: Friday morning - a passing tree broke the glass, filled the cabin with up to 5' of water, then blew the front, and lots of stuff, out. Sad day

We looked through the front sliding door, which was open, into the cabin. The door was clogged with bits of a couch, chairs, DVD cases, a lamp, a case of cameras, books and other items that once filled our home. We couldn't get through the open door. The refrigerator was stuffed beneath the bulging front wall, was open, its contents strewn here and there over the soft, brown, stinky mud that covered all of the flooring that remained. Most of the stuff we'd put on the counters - they were high enough to save those things, weren't they? - was gone. And the items Shan had put on the couches so they wouldn't get wet, including all of my compositions, journals, and a lot of piano music was also gone with the couches. The waterline was higher than the piano was tall. The piano looked ruined. We didn't try to climb over all of the debris, but saw that the side glass door was gone, that shards of broken glass were wedged into the frame that remained; the next day they sealed our plans. A large, heavy log was inside. My imagination said that the glass held until that log broke it, that water rushed in, filled the rooms, and then, when the front blew out, the water followed that easy path and took everything with it.

"This is something, huh?" I asked.

"Wow," Shan said.

Reality, it turns out, isn't as dramatic as screenwriters make it, as actors play it.

Were we surprised that the front of the house was blown out? Were we shocked? At that moment, I don't think we were. We watched the power of the flood increase all Thursday, saw many things carried off, knew by the scent how significant the damage was. The damage in the neighborhood was beyond what you'd call significant, and all sorts of stuff was still being washed away, was clogging up the bridge, sticking on trees and power poles that still stood, and so on. Shan and I knew that our place was a mere speck on the panorama of destruction. And that the world didn't revolve around us. Still, we were sad.

After our profound observations we went back up the hill to the house, where we heard Ed tell Sarah, "It's gone; it's all gone." He was shaking his head; Sarah was in shock. But quiet. As I remember it, a moment later, our hostess came into the house complaining with vigorous vitriol about a trickle of water that was running through their garage; I guess the concrete was getting wet. As I recall, no one tried to comfort her just then. There is something to be said for perspective, after all. That night, Shan heard Sarah crying quietly; Ed gently comforting her. They've been married for a long time; their commitment is strong.

Later, as we stood on the deck of the house on the high ground, Shan pointed, said, "Look! The curio is in that eddy!" The glass was smashed, and the once lovely oak cabinet - one of the very few luxury items we owned - was a wreck. I think we both wondered about the pretty items that had populated the piece, but even though we wondered about walking down and taking a look, the reality of where it was, the very heavy, deep, fast-moving water around it, and the inherent destruction water continued to wreak kept us away. (This was probably why, when people asked us when we became frightened for our lives, I always answered, "Never." We used common sense and kept our distance.) I didn't give the curio or its contents another thought; Shan mentioned a few items - *Awe, what about the?* - but didn't dwell on the loss of stuff, either. There wasn't anything we could do, anyway, so why worry.

In fact, while there was no joy in it, we knew a sense of thanksgiving. I realized that I had left my wallet in the cabin, and thought if I could find it and dry stuff out, I wouldn't have to go get new ID things: licenses, debit and credit cards, and so on. (The bears could eat the contents of the fridge, but I didn't want raccoons charging my card when they ordered pizza.) My Eagle Scout card was in there - probably the most meaningful thing - as was my Medicare card. You know, wallet stuff. We wanted to see what had happened to the items Shan piled on the bed, and I admit that I wondered how my bamboo fly rods fared.

After while, we decided to have another look at our ruined home. Shan and I walked back down the hill, then along the hill side of the cabin to our bedroom window. It was open just a little. Shan said she could open it all the way. When she started to carefully remove the screen - neither of us has experience in breaking and entering - I said, "Go ahead and rip it out; it's not like we're going to do any more damage." We both laughed. Our sense of humor had not gone or been ruined with our belongings.

"Look," said Shan, "the top of the bed is dry!" And, so was the stuff on it. "The bed must have floated!" she said.

I had waders on, and climbed through the window into the small room. "You should stay outside," I said as the waders sunk into a couple of feet of wet muck. She did. It was very difficult walking: at each step the muck tried to separate the wader from my foot! *Schluck*!

It was too wet to look for anything that was on the floor. The furniture was all upended, the bedroom door was stuck shut, but the antique chest that had been at the foot of the bed was gone. A big log was near an overturned dresser that had held my wallet and other items. I did an inventory of what I could see in order to try to determine where the wallet might be.

"Why don't you hand out some of the clothing," Shan said.

I asked her, "Is there anything here that Ed and Sarah can use?"

We looked, talked, decided, and I obeyed, handing dry items out the window to my lovely bride. And then, when I decided to follow my detective nose in an attempt to find the wallet in the mud, an interesting thing happened. It happened after I gave up on the wallet, in fact - the mud was very wet and deep; it smelled bad, too.

During the search, I saw a burnt orangey item buried in the mud. The heavy log lay adjacent to it. I realized I didn't own anything that color, and didn't think Shan had anything that color that, either. I assumed it was clothing, and the mystery of it made me curious. So I reached back into the mud and pulled it out; it made a sucking sound similar to that which the waders made. No, there was not a pop at the end. It was cloth, and looked like a canvas shirt; a shirt I'd have worn. But as I lifted it, I knew it was heavier than a wet, muddy shirt would be, and realized something was wadded up inside. My curiosity expanded beyond the shirt.

When I started to unwrap the odd shaped item that was in the shirt, I saw something white that felt solid; it was very smooth and shiny. At first, I thought it might be a big chunk of solid gold that was washed from the depths of the streambed, that it was an exceptional nugget that would pay to replace our stuff and repair the cabin. My imagination, like my sense of humor, was fully functional. Then, the reality of its whiteness and lightness cancelled the idea. As I continued to unwrap it, I saw some color, then more shape. My jaw started to drop, and my disbelief waned, when I saw that it was the Royal Dalton porcelain figurine that had been in the curio cabinet! The doll was a gift my dad purchased and had given to each of his two daughters in law, my sister and mom soon after Shan and I married. The figurine was unscathed; it's delicate foot, fan and

The pretty little figurine delicate foot and fan in tact after its adventurous ride

69

the hand that held it were complete and unmarked. I shook my head and handed it out the screenless window to Shan.

Even though we asked, we accepted the fact that regardless of how this one delicate gem escaped the cabinet, was wrapped up in a foreign canvas shirt, was flooded out of the front of the living room as the curio was swept away, washed down the hall and through the door - did it pass the chest on the way; did it ride the log? - before it was deposited in our bedroom, then buried in mud, all without a chip. At the time, standing in the stinking mud of what remained of our bedroom didn't seem the place to ask why or how questions. Instead, we laughed and cried with joy over something found!

Later, I discovered my little brown fake-leather wallet in the yucky brown mud, too. Everything inside was soaked with reeking water, and had a thin patina of fine sand; everything except the three pictures of Jessica that I carry. They were clean. Funny old flood.

During the summer of 2007, friends helped Shan and I clean out our Longmont house because we had to move to the cabin. Multiple loads of once perhaps precious items were donated, given to the help, boxed up for storage, or hauled off to and discarded at the dump. Some stuff was hard to part with. But moving from a 5,000-square foot, 3-story house to a less than 1,000-square foot, one-floor cabin meant so long to so much. We felt a sense of loss and mourned at that time, but took a deep breath and pressed on. Now, here we were again, six years later but under significantly different circumstances not of our making.

When Shan and I visited the cabin on Friday, the second day of the flood, and saw the damage, she said, "Well, I guess now we lost everything," and we laughed. (She said this after I climbed through the window and out of the bedroom.) I said, "We have a clean canvas, a new adventure. I guess we'll see what our Father has in store now!" That was the first time she mentioned Life Two, or L2.

On Friday, Marge is walking her daughter's small white cockapoo. The dog is also cute, but, as a dog, has an IQ that is dogametrically higher than Chloe's who, after all, is only a rabbit, created to be prey, to provide protein to wild canines, raptors, large reptiles and anything else in need of a meal. She and the little dog make us smile, and offer a moment's respite from our trials.

I ask Marge how she is. "This is just too much for an old lady," she says, looking down on the flood of water pushing debris along her normal dog-walk path.

I gently touch her arm. She looks back at me. Her eyes say *It is too much*, and she says again, "It's just too much for an old lady." That's not the last time she will say it, either.

I agree with her, then say, "Well, here we are."

She says, after a moment's pause, "Yes. I'm glad we are all safe." And then, as is her way, Marge smiles. She knows how.

Marge's husband of many years - both are near or past 80 - comes up, stops beside another neighbor. I hear him exclaim, while pointing over the water below, that, *The shed with twenty-thousand dollars in tools, has been washed away.* He repeats this many times that day, adding, *A lifetime of tools. My tools from when I worked for the phone company all those years.*

His eyes are a little glassy at this realization. Fair enough, don't you think? Everyone from the neighborhood was coming to grips with damage and loss.

I ask, "You had to buy your own tools?"

His eyes clear, then bore into mine as he answers, "Oh yeah."

Then, and I'm sad to say I wasn't surprised by the conspiratorial timbre of the comment, he said, "Those guys caused this," arm sweeping over the waters, "when they

71

opened the dam." (Olympus Dam near Estes Park, controlled by the Bureau of Land Management.)

I waited for a few moments and considered that statement as I looked out at the tremendous flood his arm swung over. (People who have responded to my emails have also wondered about how the opening of the dam affected damage; the media jumped on that bandwagon and stayed on for as long as it would roll.) And then I said, "No one and nothing anyone could do was going to keep this from happening."

To his credit, he stopped, thought, looked out over his still perched arm, and then bowed his head.

"I suppose not," he said as he lowered his arm. I tried to comfort him.

Friday. We looked at the damage the water had caused our neighborhood, which was all we knew, all we could see, isolated on our mountainside and cut off from the outside world as we were. After meeting Marge, hearing her *This is just too much for an old lady* several times, and trying to comfort her, Marge asked me a question. She was quite sincere. "Which do you think is worse, fire or this?"

It was a fair question because I knew that she and her husband feared fire. I think most of us did. We'd had spots of forest fires near us several times - they were put out immediately - and the nearby Storm Mountain fire in 2000 did massive destruction. (Storm Mountain is just across the street from our neighborhood, but a couple thousand feet higher in elevation.) And one dry summer day, when some people had walked up Sly Fox and started shooting lots of different weapons, Marge came by worried that the shooting would ignite a blaze. When I tried to calm her that day, her husband came to ask if I was ever in the military, told me he had been, had witnessed grass fires that started on the firing range. Of course it is difficult to comment on, let alone assuage, someone's fears.

The view from the high grounds on Thursday
By Friday, when Marge asked the question, water was higher, the
road was gone, as were most of the trees

While Marge and I stood there, I looked over the water - keep in mind that just that summer, a conflagration called the Black Forest Fire had consumed thousands of acres and hundreds of homes northeast of Colorado Springs - and said, "I suppose either is a disaster to those who are in it." Marge looked at me, thought about that, and said, "I suppose so," before she walked on with her daughter's little white dog.

Since the flood, I've been thinking about the comparison, fire and water, wondering about the differences between them. The first reported destruction of the world, and almost every living thing on it, occurred after Noah obeyed God and built the ark. It rained; the Earth flooded. The last, final destruction of the world, its system and the evil it supports, will come by fire, according to Biblical prophecy. I think then, the only ark will be faith in Jesus, that His saving grace will be for everyone who calls His name. Everything else will burn.

The pictures we saw after the Black Forest Fire showed a few bits of brick rubble where a home once stood; there wasn't any rubble where Ed and Sarah's house had been.

We saw pictures of auto carcasses, burned to their frames, but I never found my truck. Still, there were many vehicle skeletons along the river, some stuck under bridges, others wrapped around trees; several were scattered around our neighborhood. In other words, both uncontrolled fire and too much water cause significant damage that cannot be undone; both consume. The old is gone, all the way gone, and it can only be replaced with the new.

Because there is no fixing that which is gone. There is usually no fixing that which is wrong, either. I learned this while teaching piano lessons. When a student practiced an incorrect note, rhythm, fingering, etcetera, there was no fixing the error. And good wrong practice, like good correct practice, works: the mistake is as solid as are all that is correct around it. The mistake can be played with musicality and artistry; but it's still a mistake: it's not what the composer intended.

The only way to play the correct note is to discard the wrong one and replace it with the correct one.

Pretty much like God, in Jesus, replaces death - everyone is born dead - with Life.

B rittany sent this e-mail on Friday, September 13.

Hello Everyone!

I thought I would send out an update to let you know what we know about my parents. Yesterday they called my Pattison Grandparents and said that the water in the house was mid-calf. They put things up on the counter and bed to (hopefully) stay dry. They went up to a friend's house who lives up the hill behind them. They took Max and Chloe the bunny with them. Since it did not stop raining all night we hope that the water levels did not go up a whole lot more, but it sounds like they may have.

We have not heard from them today and probably won't as all phone and electrical lines are down. A bridge in the narrows has collapsed and the road above them to Estes has also caved (this all happened yesterday morning) as well as bridges/roads up towards Glen Haven so I'm thinking they may get a free helicopter ride out of the deal! (Just what they were hoping for I'm sure)

Anyway, as I know anything substantial I will pass it along to you all. Thank you for the prayers! We (Jess, Rachel, and I) all feel confident that they are safe. I'm sure spending multiple days with all the neighborhood in two homes will be an adventure!

Thanks for being friends to our family and parents! We love you!

Brittany Meek (the middle daughter) (and probably Rachel and Jess as well)

Brittany's emails circulated, were forwarded and read by family, friends and acquaintances of each; we didn't find out until after the free helicopter ride.

EVACUATED

The festivities ended up being too much for Caleb, at age 5 the youngest of our stranded gathering. Once the rain stopped and being out-of-doors became inviting, Caleb expressed pure and unadulterated little boy energy! He ran up and down the hill, yelled his observations, threw things in the water, and worried his folks and neighbors when he got too close to it at the bottom of Sly Fox Road. Everyone kept their eyes peeled for Caleb, while they watched and listened to his enthusiasm. Caleb, like Miss Bunny, brought smiles to most faces. Kids see things differently.

His enthusiasm lasted through Saturday morning when Caleb ran out of energy, and felt ill. He'd had enough. He wasn't alone.

All of us were in various stages of shock, fatigue, filth and emotional exhaustion. Tempers flared, and old habits of irrational relations arose once again. As Caleb and the rest of us wore out that Saturday morning, we were also aware that the flood waters were receding. The lower water revealed damage to the area, made it clearer to all of us. Almost all of the topsoil and everything it held was gone, along with trees and other vegetation, replaced by boulders, stones, rocks, sand, tree trunks and so on. The original riverbed was full of debris and the water flowed through a new course of its own making, the one it apparently preferred. Many helicopters chopped through and disturbed the air, replacing the roar of flood water and grinding boulders with the whirl of blades. We wondered when one would land, and waited.

As the water began to abate, the neighbors started to get concerned about how much fresh water we had, but more so about the two elderly couples. One of the wives required a constant source of oxygen, and the other husband needed it at night, but had given all of his supply to his neighbor.

By this time one of Rodney's friends had climbed over the mountain to see how we were. A volunteer firefighter, he had walkie-talkies that were tuned to the frequency of similar devices others in the canyon had, and gave one to Rodney. Soon after, a telephone company chopper landed on what remained of County Road 43. People crowded around; three men disembarked and carried on a conversation. After a few minutes, two men stayed as the pilot lifted off and flew to a spot near the post office where several people were stranded. They climbed aboard and the chopper lifted off and disappeared over the mountain.

The evacuation had begun. Tears of hope flowed. Discussions mixed with arguments ensued concerning where a chopper would land in our neighborhood. A few threats of bodily harm were made. Rodney called someone who was on CR 43 to tell them we needed to evacuate two elderly couples as soon as possible; we waited.

A while later - I haven't worn or obeyed a watch for nearly forty years - the same helicopter returned and landed on CR 43. We waited. A few moments later it lifted off, flew in our direction, hovered while the pilot did an inventory of the area, then landed on a gravel bar near the CDOT building. Water flowed through channels on all sides of the spot. There was no question in any of our minds concerning who would get on the first flight, and everyone assisted our elderly friends down the muddy hill to the LZ. Someone used a handy section of guard rail to construct a bridge across the narrowest channel. Two men carried Carolyn while others toted bags for all four people. Once loaded, waves, smiles and tears sent them on their way as the helicopter lifted off, then flew over the mountain.

Our first set of evacuees lifts off over the little island LZ

We waited and wondered. A group of people at least as large as ours formed near CR 43. We all knew that many other individuals and groups would be isolated along the canyon, in need of evacuation. Numerous flights of various types of helicopters continued to fly overhead.

While Shan and I waited, we decided to take another look at the cabin. Ed and Gabriel helped us remove the items from the bed, as well as a few other things that looked dry and salvageable. One of the high grounds neighbors had agreed to let us store a few items in their shed, and

Ed and Gabriel humped all of it up the hill for us. After that was done, Shan decided we should make another pass through the place. We hadn't yet been in any part other than the bedroom - the front door was blocked, and up until that time the opening where the side door had been had deep, powerful water rushing past. The back door had four feet of wet, muddy sand packed against it.

We climbed through the bedroom window, forced open the door, which was held shut by mud and other debris, and walked on the mud and sand through the cabin. What a mess. After our reconnaissance, we went into the kitchen/dining area. Then, Shan walked to the opening where the side sliding glass door had been and looked out.

"Turn this way," I said. She did. I snapped a few photos of the view through the door, across the street to where Ed's and Sarah's house had been, where the river now flowed through what had been our yard and River Fork Road, following the same path it described early Thursday morning, only much deeper and with no vegetation.

After I snapped the shots, Shan turned, looked down at the rubble that was far below the level the deck had occupied, grabbed the door frame and jumped out the door. Glass shards gashed her hand. I was following, my head down so as not to stumble on pots, pans and other ruined things embedded in the mud, when I heard her say, "Uh oh."

When I looked out the door, she was looking down at her left hand, palm up, which was cradled in her right hand. She said, "I cut my hand."

As I climbed down, I asked, "How bad?"

"It's pretty deep," she said. I confirmed this for myself when I took a look. Shan remained calm.

After I went back into the cabin and raided the medicine cabinet - happily, gauze and antiseptic ointments were dry - mixed emotions surged through both of our hearts and

Shan poses inside for a photo - water still roaring
A moment later, Shan poses while holding her severely cut hand, surrounded by raging water and massive destruction

minds as we walked through massive amounts and varieties of rubble along the side, then the front of the cabin, and up the hill to where we had been staying.

Once there, we found a remaining bottle of water, washed the very deep, nasty-looking gash that traversed her hand from between her ring finger and pinky to the heel of her hand, cleaned it as we could, applied ointment, and then used bandages to create several butterflies to hold it shut before covering it thoroughly with the gauze. Calm Sarah helped. Once again, I was happy with Boy Scout and other first aid training I'd received. Shan was brave and without any form of hysteria.

"You knucklehead," I lovingly said to her when the wound work was complete.

"I didn't even notice the glass," she said.

"Accidents happen," I said. And then we laughed.

"It's going to take twenty stitches," I announced. Shan rolled her eyes.

News of the injury circulated fast, and Rodney called for a medical evacuation, saying we had an injury that needed attention. At the time, I figured they'd take Shan and that I'd have to stay behind. As events unfolded, it was clear that

On the Apache: Max, Chloe (in the bag) Shan, Caleb and Joy

worn out Caleb had to be flown out, and of course his mom, Joy, would go along. They packed bags; we assembled a few items for Shan; everyone waited. Within a relatively short time a National Guard UH-60 Black Hawk helicopter landed on CR 43; a moment later it lifted off and flew to our LZ.

While the chopper came our way, "Dale!" Rodney yelled, "get your stuff; you're going with Shan!" Others agreed; it

was a surprise to me. I went up the hill, gathered what I could from where we stayed - this included Max; Lily brought Chloe, who we put in a backpack - and hurried down the hill to the helicopter.

Several people helped me across the guard rail bridge. Chris' boyfriend carried Max, wading across the thigh-deep muddy water. I climbed aboard, joining Shan, Joy and Caleb. We waved a quick *so long*, and

80

the pilot flew us away. I snapped photos. Shan cried. Joy had fallen on the way to the LZ and was bruised and bleeding, but smiled. So did Caleb: *I'm flying in a helicopter!*

It was loud, but smooth. We flew downstream less than a mile. A CH-47 Chinook hovered there, the back wheels and huge rearward-facing door over remaining asphalt, the front hovering over the maw of the river. National Guardsmen hurried and directed us from the Black Hawk into the Chinook, where other canyon neighbors I recognized were seated. Bottles of water were distributed with snacks and ear plugs. Eyes were cloudy. Faces blended looks of terror and pending relief. Honesty was apparent.

Crates held dogs; people held cats. Chloe, nestled in her backpack burrow, was as happy as a bunny could be. Max was nervous, and stood by where I sat, leaning against my legs. Shan, Joy and Caleb clutched bags, buckled into their seats, and everyone waited until security was confirmed. The huge chopper rattled a little as it lifted off. It was very loud; everyone inserted the ear plugs. The noise must have hurt Max and the other pets' ears.

We observed new damage that was so much more, as ours would be to others. Eyes peered out windows, but heads soon bowed as the enormity of it all continued its relentless

We transferred to this Chinook for the rest of the ride out

attack. I tried to catch others' glances, to share a smile of encouragement, as is my wont. Shan held her injured hand and smiled back. I think she was experiencing a modicum of shock, but not so much that would influence her inward faith and the thankfulness that springs from it.

After a short circuit down a length of canyon, the chopper lifted higher into the air, flew over dry ground, the foothills and Horsetooth Reservoir that separated us from our homes and the landing and collecting area west of Ft. Collins. On arrival we noticed other recently landed, still running Chinooks and more helicopters unlading their burden of dry but emotionally sodden people. We were rushed out of our own vehicle, met by wild land firefighter volunteers, and herded to waiting school busses. Pallets of bottled water and piles of snacks lined the way. People offered help. We removed the ear plugs. I hoped my head would clear.

When we arrived at the bus, someone asked our names and recorded them on a list. We were now on the roles of the rescued, entered in the realm of victimhood.

LZ east of Horesetooth Reservoir near Ft. Collins
was a flurry of activity, with volunteers, busses, crates of water and
snacks, and people asking a lot of questions

EVACUATION

On that Saturday, September 14, 2013, these emails went out.

Hey Everyone,

Thank you for your prayers and well wishes. For those of you that have emailed me, I'm sorry I haven't been able to write back. In addition to all that has gone on I worked last night until after midnight and then this morning until 2:00. Anyway, here is the newest update. One of mom and dad's neighbors has been rescued and said that everyone from the neighborhood is fine. Praise the Lord! Mom and Dad are OK and pets are being rescued along with people so Max and Chloe will also be able to come out of the canyon.

Sadly, the Egloff's house (across the street from mom and dad) and the cabin (mom and dad's house) are both completely gone. Some good family friends in Longmont have said that mom and dad can stay with them for as long as needed. We're very thankful for all the support from everyone. It has definitely been quite the past few days and Rachel, Jess, and I (along with our grandparents) are all looking forward to hearing mom and dad's voices. In pictures it looks like the Subaru and Nissan might be OK, so that is good. Though it will probably be a bit before they are able to drive out of the canyon.

Thanks again for all your support. Maybe the next update will be from my dad!

Love you all!

Brittany (and Rachel and Jessica)

And a little later, Brittany added:

Hello all!

Mom and Dad are with Jessica in Fort Collins. Mom cut her hand and will need stitches, but other than that they're fine! Dad also said that some of cabin is still there! The piano is all muddy and the truck floated down the river with dad's best fishing gear. So keep your eyes peeled for a maroon truck!

This will be the last of my updates, but feel free to e-mail me or call me if you have any questions. Thank you everyone for all your support! The journey has just begun.

Blessed be the name of the Lord.

Brittany

The bus ride was non-eventful. The bus was full of people who varied in age. Each person had a different mien that expressed something from adventure, relief, sadness, fear and so on. Dogs, cats, a bowl of fish and another with a snake rode along. Max, after so much standing, settled and laid down on the floor by my feet. Bunny, still clueless, remained snug in the backpack.

Shan rides the bus
"Not yet, it isn't!"

At one point, I reached over the seat back that separated Shan and me and said, "Smile; it's time to be happy."

As she began to cry and her tears flowed down her beautiful face to a sad frown, she said, "Not yet it isn't."

Within a few moments of getting off the bus that we rode from the Ft. Collins landing area to the church collection area, a Denver Post reporter started asking Shan questions of the this-is-what-I-want-to-hear-from-you persuasion reporters practice in order to get the predetermined story they want to write. Shan, ever patient and kind, wanted to hug Jessica and Robert, Ed and Sarah's anxious son, needed to have her hand tended to, complied and answered the questions. The next day, the paper ran a story that pretentiously interpreted what the reporter assumed was the kids' anxiety, Jess' reunion with her bunny, and so on. People sent us links and hard copies. Whoopee for celebrity!."

Later, but not until after our pets were welcomed with treats and open arms, we were shuffled into the large host church. We passed right through the registration area when we announced Shan's need for immediate medical attention. Both Shan and Joy, who had abrasions suffered when she fell on the way to the helicopter, were pointed to the Red Cross aid station. A lot of people wearing Red Cross vests milled around, but no one seemed to know what to do. A particularly bossy woman bossed people, who stood around looking forlorn and confused. But one person seemed to be a genuine medical person. Yes, the others probably meant well, were kind and properly concerned, but the volunteer nurse, who we later discovered was a member of the church rather than of the Red Cross, got right to quietly and effectively defusing the minor drama when she cleaned and temporarily treated Shan's wound. Then, while other people discussed and importantly pontificated about where Shan and Joy should or should not go for treatment - there was no talk of how we might get there, mind you - our gentle registered nurse took Joy and Caleb, Shan and I aside and said she would drive us to an urgent care center she knew. And she did. She also stayed with us until the girls were completely treated. (I wonder who took her place back at the aid station?)

In between our arrival at and departure from the stitching place, our new friend and I shared a few stories and became

Shan and Caleb
on the way to urgent care

better acquainted. She talked on the phone with Jessica - who had been unceremoniously left behind, confused and alone at the church with Max and Chloe - and explained where we were and how to get there. I still feel awful about leaving Jess like that. Like others we met, in our focus to do a right we also did a wrong.

When Jessica got to the urgent care facility, I knew she wanted to see her mom, that her mom wanted to see her, so Jess went into the operatory to watch the skilled PA stitch Shan's wound. It was a curious, but excellent, reunion. They visited. Afterwards, Shan showed our RN the job and related a story an aid had shared after the wound was stitched, saying, "She told me that even though he's not an MD, John is the very best sewer they have." Our RN said it looked very nice, and the way it healed bears witness to the work and the narrative.

Friends came to pick up Joy and Caleb, and after much hugging and many best wishes our gentle RN drove Shan and I back to the church. Jess followed in her car. Jess had explained that someone who lived near the church offered to watch Max, and that a small animal hospital took Chloe. When things settled and we were ready, we could call and retrieve the pets. The next day, Jess' boyfriend, Blake, took Max to his apartment in Ft. Collins; a few days later we got some of the best, most heartening news we'd yet received when Jessica reported that her apartment manager had told her, *Of course you can keep your bunny here!* Tears were shed at the news. Max stayed with Blake, and Tyco the boxer, until we moved onto the Farm. He's still adapting, but likes being with us and romping the open spaces with Kep and Sis, the farm's resident dogs. Chasing chickens was a bonus he gave up after a few days.

Back at Timberline Church, pets settled, wound sutured, we were told to register. They asked if we'd informed a certain group that we were off the mountain. Shan told them that, after the helicopter ride and as we were boarding the bus, someone was taking everyone's names. (Earlier, I think it was Shan's mom, in Ohio, had called to report us missing.) Shan then related that on the bus ride, just moments after Shan had given the person our names, Shan's friend Tammy called Shan's cell phone to say she saw that we'd been rescued. Amazing, huh?

Once the paperwork was complete, we were told there was food and shelter in Auditorium C, that a meeting with the Sheriff, Red Cross and representatives of other entities would begin at 7 p.m. in Auditorium D. Since we'd climbed on the helicopter an hour or two earlier, there had been nothing but a scurry of activity. It was moderately exhausting when piled on the rest.

"Where's the food," I asked.

While a few volunteers tried to tell us how to get to where the food was being served, pointing and arguing with one another about directions, another said, "Follow me."

A multitude of volunteers wandered the halls. Many congregated in small knots, apparently unsure of what to do, what to say. A few were overtly outgoing, but not very helpful, while others were compassionate and knew they were there to provide assistance according to the need of the person they endeavored to serve. Like our *follow me* fellow.

One of the Gospel authors reports that several religious people passed by a severely beaten man, until one man had compassion and helped the injured man. Concern can watch someone die; compassion acts and provides aid to the one in need. We observed both concern and inaction, compassion and action. Being a servant and serving is about the one in need; it's not the other way around; it's not about personal accolades.

The food, donated by a local Olive Garden restaurant, consisted of salad, pasta, bread, various drinks and a table of deserts. At the small serving counter, too many volunteers seemed to get in the way of the hungry rescued. There was confusion, which, even at the time, seemed fair enough. I doubt that very many - volunteers or rescued - had practiced or prepared for this big show, that anyone was reading from a script.

The tables where "victims" sat to eat were different. The poignant rescue drama complete, shock set in and continued to ruminate: I could see it in many eyes, on many faces. Disheveled, dirty clothes hung from many drooping shoulders while small plastic forks full of food were lifted to less than receptive mouths. We were hungry but had no appetite for eating. Even while they ate, the rescued expressed their loss with honesty. Some had lost friends or a family member, were unsure of the safety of others, lost pets, homes and belongings, and any sense of security they'd found in all of it. I wanted to encourage, as is my wont, but had the need to eat, too. It was time for a smile and a knowing nod; it wasn't time to pontificate philosophically. I think volunteers sensed this, too, because most kept their distance while they circled the tables, perhaps unsure of how to respond to such raw grief. Eye contact became an invitation to join, but little was made.

Others who were rescued ate and shared stories of rising water, of the dawning realization it would keep getting higher, and their response to it: what they did, how they got out, and so on. Over and again on the loudspeaker, different folks announced the impending meeting in Auditorium D that would begin in fifteen minutes, then ten, then five, and so on.

After we finished eating, Shan and I wandered out of the dining/shelter area in Auditorium C. I saw the *follow me* volunteer who had led us to the food, walked to him and asked, "I suppose you know the way to the meeting hall, too?" He laughed - we'd already shared a few friendly digs - and said, "Right this way."

Our first post-rescue meal was over, other than the post-meeting dessert Shan fetched later. We were off the mountain, safe with our dear Jessica, Max and Chloe and a few of our neighbors. Shan's wound was sewn, and we were on our way to hear what might be next. The clean canvas was ready for the first few brush strokes of L2.

The 7 p.m. meeting in Auditorium D, in spite of the announcements, started late. Shan and I sat and waited at a round table towards the back of the hall - I've been a back row end sitter for many years, preferring access to quiet escape when required. While we waited, we had two sets of visitors. The first were two women wearing Larimer County Sheriff's Office vests. An official looking name tag announced that they were victim's advocates.

The shorter of the duo was more assertive than her taller companion, who seemed mild and meek. Within a few moments I saw why. The assertive one, who was demanding in her insistent help, dominated as she began pouring assumptions on us concerning how much we must hurt and how much she must help. The deluge was primarily aimed at Shan, who was vulnerable, and cried. But the tears weren't for herself, about how she actually felt so much, as for the ideas of victimhood so clearly expressed by the

89

assertive victim's advocate, who, fed by Shan's tears and show of emotion, continued to pile on platitudes of pain and suffering. Who knew that an advocate was supposed to sew grief in order to increase their own harvest? The tall woman remained quiet and appeared to become more ill at ease. When I finally started to confront one of what I thought was a particularly poignant of many asinine assumptions stated by the shorter advocate - it was the statement having to do with being frightened by the unknown - Shan shushed me. This was the first manifestation of the supposed-to-be-comforted one having to comfort the supposed-to-be-comforter. (In this case, dear Shan was trying to protect the advocate from my comments.) Once again, in deference to Shan, I swallowed my own emotions and yielded to Shan's and, in this case, that of another.

Early on, I was aware of pent up emotions which I was not allowed to express. (The angst continued for many months; writing this book served as my only outlet. Editing has stirred up troubling thoughts and memories that inspire strong emotions for me and Shan.)

While the short advocate continued to pour salt on our open wounds - I felt sorry for the tall woman - three more people came and sat down at the table. There were two women and one man. When the advocates, apparently finished with advocacy on our behalf, left to hunt other victims, the older of the two women took over. She asked, "Were you rescued?" and Shan told her we'd been flown out a few hours earlier.

I don't remember the specifics of the older woman's speech - it turned out to be more selfish pontificatory crap, and so much noise, my ears didn't care to hear or to even listen - but I remember the man, who seemed to be her husband, looked embarrassed by her rudeness, and took on an *I am so sorry* look in his eyes that did nothing to stop her mucky gibberish. It was like his wife was bragging about how delightful her new perfume smelled, but he knew she'd smeared her hair with fresh dog shit. The other woman was equally submissive, perhaps used to being squelched by her friend's tirades. Neither tried to stay her, and before I asked her to stop - I hesitated, wondering if Shan would shush me again - she made a final banal announcement, stood, looked down her nose at us, shook her head and left. The others followed, as though in tow, heads bowed.

Psalm 69: 1-3 Save me, O God! For the waters have come up to my neck. I sink in deep mire, where there is no standing; I have come into deep waters, where the floods overflow me.

Now I have no idea where people such as the short Sheriff Advocate's or Gabby Older Woman's hearts were, to whom they listened, or where the voices they listened to and just knew had to be obeyed came from. Maybe they scripted the words they said to each and every victim they met. I still don't. And I'm not judging them, even though my comments could be so construed due to their angry timbre. (I was irate.) I think there is a difference between discernment and judgment, and am pretty sure these two, and similar types we met, neither understood nor exercised discernment but manifested judgment full speed ahead, when they imposed their judgment of what they assumed was our need. If they thought they were being helpful and felt good about themselves as a result of their interaction with us, well, I suppose that's fine. In fact, I think it was the point from their perspective: they wanted to feel good about themselves. In spite of all that, they were the source of the flood mentioned by the Psalmist in the above quote, as far as I was concerned. Most of the time I'm an optimist, but that turns to skeptical optimism when I meet thoughtless people like them, or people who listen only to themselves.

Is make self feel good the point? It often seems so. Before the meeting started, and while the two women assaulted us with their agendas, the overspreading cloth of Western Materialistic Subjective Nihilism - that's a mouthful - and its concern for self allowed no room for compassion. I think this is because concern comes first for so many people, that most of their concern is for themselves.

However, like the still small voice of God, compassion is out there. In the midst of the noise of the multitudes, of the media and others, Shan and I heard Him and knew His Grace, often as expressed and made manifest in the decent, compassionate acts of others, including family, friends and complete strangers we trusted.

We witnessed just such an act of compassion from a stranger when the meeting actually started. Following the prelude and introductions, Larimer County Sheriff Justin Smith walked to the stage, was introduced, and stood at the podium before speaking into the microphone. As he began to address the mixed gathering of rescued and volunteers, he spoke as to a group of individuals who he knew were experiencing varying degrees of shock. I could tell that he was, too. He said, "First, I do not see any of you as victims, but as survivors!" The survivors spontaneously, but quietly and without much energy, cheered to hear it, too. Apart from the muted, but sincere, enthusiasm - we were all tired - it sounded as though many shared my dislike of forced-upon victimhood!

Then, the Sheriff explained his agenda. First and foremost, searches and evacuations continued and wouldn't end until every person was accounted for. There was another cheer. He announced that there were fatalities but in no way demeaned those lost by making comparisons to the significant loss of life (144 killed) caused by the 1976 Big Thompson Flood. The man was grieving - I could hear it in his voice, see it in his demeanor - while tirelessly doing his job. I found a sense of relief and small security in the leadership Sheriff

Smith projected. He continued making precise statements concerning damage, saying other issues would be addressed once everyone was evacuated. He encouraged each of us to register and take assistance from available relief organizations before announcing that he had work to do. But before he departed, this kind, exhausted man encouraged each of us, drawing from the deep well of character true leaders possess. He provided soothing salve to our shock, our pain.

When the meeting was over, after others from various entities addressed the crowd, Shan turned to me as someone walked past with a piece of cake, and asked, "Did you know there was desert?"

"Yes."

"Want some?"

"Chocolate cake, please," I said.

As Shan stood to go in search of desert, church volunteers began closing and stacking folding chairs and tables in the auditorium. I sat, watched and listened. When Shan returned with sweet delicacies, we sat at our table and ate while the scurry of activity rattled on nearby. I observed a sense of tactile purpose as people folded, carried and stacked tables and chairs, which submitted and obeyed the energy imposed on them. (Our advocate was not pleased when I rejected and questioned hers on me.) It was a physical labor with immediate, tangible results, that was unlike the long term recovery we and many others faced.

We hadn't been able to avoid what the water thrust on us. We'd been like those chairs and tables. Even though we had volition they didn't have, our willfulness did nothing to stop the relentless rising water. The water did water very well, in obedience to gravity and the truth of physical law, as it rose and destroyed things in its path.

My opinion of the flood has, nor had, any bearing on the rising water and what it did. Nothing I could do, think or say would divert, slow, lower or otherwise change the course of the water. And my opinion of Truth, of God's love and grace, has no bearing on Him, on what He will do. I can neither help nor harm the flow of history, or anything that was created, or is sustained, by His power.

And now, Shan and I, and many others, are faced with the same, ongoing question: *How shall we then live?* Of course the loud, persistent, and at times angry question we've been asked most is, *What are you going to do now?* or, *So, how are you doing?* or, the less personal but ever popular, *How's it going?*

Early on, I built an e-mail list of people who I knew cared or thought would be interested in what was going on. Then, I composed and sent notes to inform family and friends about what was going on. Man, was e-mail a blessing for communicating! Phone calls became exhausting due to the rudeness of some; and I became fatigued by the repetitive nature calls assumed with friends and family. (We were also low on cell minutes.) In most cases, I attached pictures to illuminate what I wrote. I also duplicated and posted the notes and most of the photos on a fly tying web site I've participated in for several years.

As word got out, the outpouring of love, encouragement and tangible help that people gave has been much better than the flood of water. No one expressed more compassion than my brother, Don.

On Sunday morning, September 15, when we thought we were settled for awhile at a friend's place, I composed and sent this e-mail. I attached additional pictures that I'd taken on Thursday, Friday and Saturday while we were still on the mountain. It tells the story.

Hi,

I've tried to include everyone who sent an e-mail, but who knows?

The last one I sent was early Thursday morning. Most of you, who have watched news reports, know more than we do because shortly after that e-mail our electric and phones went out. More would follow.

Early - before 6 a.m. - we knew there was trouble flowing. Shan and I moved the cars and I convinced 2 neighbors to drive a vehicle across the bridge. Shortly after, someone towed them from where we'd parked, and as far as we know they are all over there. Getting to them will take months, if not more.

For several hours I waded on our deck in fast rushing knee deep water trying to keep the water from coming in the sliding door. As is the case with humans and other living things God made, we have a certain sense of hope and optimism, so we thought the water couldn't rise any more. So much for our prophetic propensities, as you'll note.

We stayed in the cabin until early afternoon. Shan packed a few clothes and odds and ends, I got my computer and backup drives, and we took Max up the hill to a neighbors who asked us to stay there. Chloe, the rabbit, was in her cage on the couch. After a short time, a neighbor went with Shan back to the cabin. The water was much higher. They grabbed the cage, bunny within, as the water reached the top of the couch. Bunny stayed with another neighbor, who pampered her! Max was with us, and believe it or not, behaved.

Later Thursday, but still while light as the rain continued falling, my truck went past, then the big Colorado Spruce, the deck and so on. Someone said they saw a body. [I don't think this was true.]

On Friday morning the water was much higher, but the rain stopped. It was a matter of how long it would take for what had fallen to run off the mountains and down the stream. Our neighbors across the road lost their entire house, both of their cars. Another neighbor's house was washed out; almost everyone in the low area lost their vehicles, trailers, campers, motor homes and parts of their houses. The riverbed and harshest flow ended up in what had been our front yard and the street out front. The bridge was stuffed with sand and debris, and as the water fell none was flowing in the original streambed.

During that day, our normally irrationally behaving neighbors liked one another; people shared. Much was done for the 2 elderly couples, including great lengths to move Carolyn and make sure she got oxygen. It involved breaking into another little camper that had a generator, jumping the vehicle so the generator worked in order to make O2 with her condenser.

By Saturday morning, several folks were threatening to kill one another, making for a peculiar sense of unrest. And then, a firefighter from down canyon hiked over the mountain and brought a walkie-talkie that was on line with another fire fighter just across the river on the Glen Haven Road. That fellow was able to communicate with the folks who flew in on the first helicopter, a phone company crew checking their equipment, doing inventory.

After talking - we knew not what about - the chopper lifted off, flew to the Post Office where a small dry spot sheltered several stranded folks. It evacuated them; we cheered. When the copter returned and heard of our elderly couples, they flew to a drying area of rubble - see pix - and the 4 of them were taken out. We cried with joy!

Later - about noon - Shan and I and a few others decided to see what we could find in the cabin. A couple from on the hill said we could put some stuff in their shed. We collected some things, and then Shan decided to look out the main sliding glass door - now totally gone. I took a picture, and for some reason she held onto the frame, which was full of glass shards. When she turned to jump out to where the deck, flowers and so on used to be, her hand slid down the frame and her hand was badly cut.

I cleaned it and fixed it as I could, then told the walkie-talkie holder that Shan needed stitches - I guessed 20 would do it. He called across, said a medical evacuation was needed, and within a short time a National Guard medical chopper appeared. Everyone insisted I go with her, so I got my bag and computer stuff. The neighbor with the bunny brought her out; we put her in a pack, carried Max and the stuff onto the chopper and took off. Shan wept with relief that I was with her, which was fair enough. I guess after 35 years she's partially addicted to my presence; imagine that.

We flew downstream about 1/2 mile and landed on a piece of road that was still there. A Chinook awaited us, and everyone and everything were trundled into the belly of that monster. A short flight over Storm Mountain and Horsetooth Res brought us to the landing zone, where we loaded into a bus. Max relaxed, laid on the floor and closed his eyes. Shan was emotional and felt sad - as you can see.

When we arrived at the church that was hosting the festivities, Jessica was waiting with Robert, our neighbors' son. We filled him in on the condition of his folks, told him about the house being gone, and asked him to take Max on a walk so he could pee. Jess put bunny in a cat carrier - the first thing was about pets (?) and then we went to the Aid room.

A very kind RN was mixed in with Red Cross volunteers. She further cleaned the injury, then drove Shan and I, our neighbor Joy who was injured walking to the chopper and her young son, Caleb, to an urgent care facility. Both Joy and Shan were taken in within moments, and a skilled doc put 20 (!) stitches into Shan's hand. It looks great. No nerves or other major things were damaged - I'll take them out in 7-10 days, when it's clearly mended.

Jess gave us her car, and we drove to a friend's place in Loveland where we will be for a few days.

No idea about many things. Hopefully this info will clear a few things.

I'll answer emails as I will answer them, so don't take anything personally if I don't answer yours immediately. Right now, there is no immediately for me. Our stuff is now all gone, and we have no idea how anything is going to work its way out.

Most of you know the stuff doesn't matter to me, so there's no reason to waste energy worrying about....anything.

Thanks for caring. Shan and I thank you for caring, for those of you who really pray. If you would like to forward this to groups you know we are/have been involved with so they know - thanks!

For now, we're tired and fatigued, but very well and full of hope and joy.

Love,

dale & Shan

That Sunday, we *were* tired and felt fatigued, and we also had a sense of relief after being relieved of the adventure on the mountain. We didn't have many questions at that time, and we had no answers. Many emails came in response.

As time plodded on over the first few days after we were evacuated, the sound, vibration and roar of the water continued in my mind's ear, within my bones and innards. The putrid scent still lingered in my olfactory system. It seemed like they would never stop, like the gentle rocking of being on a boat persists after disembarking. For some reason, I was reminded of a Brazilian girl who worked in Belize for a friend of mine who ran dive trips. Her job was scheduling trips, and it involved boats, lots of boats. When she was going to leave San Pedro, she told me, "I will never again work for a business that depends on boats."

A few days later, when I visited the Federal Emergency Management Agency (FEMA) and Small Business Administration (SBA) office in Loveland, I met the couple who owned the Indian Village store down river from Drake. They'd lived there in '76, as well, but the store and their house survived that flood. This time, I knew their place - store, home, two RVs and horses - was gone. We visited, talked, shared. They were mature and clear. I asked, "Any thoughts about what you might do?"

She said, "All I know is we won't build on a river again."

CALLS FOR ASSISTANCE

On Monday, our second day out, I called to register with FEMA, the first contact entity suggested, from the Coffee Tree in downtown Loveland. (Before moving from the cabin to Loveland, Jessica, our youngest daughter, applied for a job and was hired to work at this delightful coffee shop. Her bosses gave us a gift certificate the first time we stopped in after being evacuated, knowing we needed internet access and a place to hang out. I've been there almost every day since.) The fellow who answered at FEMA spoke in a difficult-to-understand accent; my poor hearing didn't help. We went through the info; I often had to ask him to repeat questions, and he my answers. But we eventually finished and the information was recorded on a computer. Before hanging up, I asked where he had been born. He said, "Guinea. I'll bet you don't know where it is." I said there were two in northeast South America, one in Africa, and one in the Pacific. He was surprised. He asked, "Which part of Africa?" and I answered *West Africa*, which further surprised him. My mind was clear, which kept my jumbled emotions in check.

More phone calls to FEMA's internet tech support followed, until the promised contact with them via the internet was opened. I found helpful, clear-speaking people, and their opposites, during phone calls and visits to the FEMA center in Loveland. I think many workers there - at least the ones I spoke with - must have been contractors hired to collect information. They were not helpful, even when they obviously tried to be, and dispensed what was inaccurate information. Later, I was delighted to find James, who was stationed in the Denver FEMA office. He was interested, precise, kind, clear, encouraging and caring. This was a significant change from FEMA employees who answered the help line, who were rude, crass people who apparently only read from a computer screen - often poorly

- and didn't care a lick, refused to listen to what I said, could not answer the questions I asked.

I also spoke with representatives from other groups, and over time, received a variety of answers to the same questions. People within a particular organization didn't know what others within the same one had said. In some cases, I was treated with outright contempt, given what I knew was inaccurate information because I'd heard what had already proved to be true from another in the same organization. And sister, or related, organizations didn't know what others were doing, either. There was a lot of *I*, but very little *TEAM*. When people who were actually working together within the same organization asked me to answer questions that they should have either known or discovered on their own, I became very frustrated. I wasn't surprised, because trying to deal with people who neither listen nor think *is* frustrating! I tried to keep Shan away from these conversations to protect her from the confusing contemptuousness I often encountered. It wasn't something she needed, on top of the rest. Rudely presented misinformation is tough to handle on the best of days when one's humor is intact.

In retrospect, though, I've decided that government and other entities need people to fill positions that don't require clear thought or much else in the way of compassionate common sense. I suppose it keeps people off of unemployment rolls. Do politicians and MBAs who create these agencies know a thing about how they operate? Would they approve? Of course they are isolated from the day-to-day stuff, like "big box" stores that fill positions with people who are neither knowledgeable about products nor helpful to customers. Government and the big box: required, but often distasteful, intrinsically demeaning pieces of American culture.

The second mass e-mail was sent on Monday afternoon, September 16. While a few things seemed to be coming together, many turned to mucky goo and ended up taking months to settle. (In fact, most remain unresolved as I edit this again in April, then May, 2014.)

Hello again!

It's the e-mail pest saying hello from dry Loveland. The sun is out; the rain has stopped. Pretty neat. And the sound of rushing waters, the vibration of tumbling boulders and so on are gone, other than in my shallow head.

Shan and I are moderately overwhelmed with emails and phone calls and messages. I've endeavored to answer both, but if you were missed I hope you won't take it personally.

This morning we started making lists of what to do. I began with short term items, including a phone charger. Shan got a PO Box in Loveland so we can get mail, has been in contact with insurance companies. I spent an enjoyable hour speaking with 2 different FEMA folks who said we'll have a call from an inspector within a day or so. I guess we'll figure out what happens next on this.

We bought some groceries, 2 used shirts and a pair of socks for me, and probably a few other things. We went to a breakfast place that I usually enjoy, but the plate came and everything was cold. You know, I really wanted a hot meal, and for the first time I snapped at the waitress, saying that I really wanted hot food. Interesting.

Thanks to all of you for your compassion or concern, and the offers. Quite frankly, the concept of accepting, receiving is mostly foreign to me because, as it turns out, I'm a net giver. I think something is happening, though. I remember standing in the rain, watching stuff float past in the roaring torrent and saying to Shan, "You know, I suppose I'll have to be prepared to accept a few things." Of course, she smiled at me and nodded, perhaps feeling a similar sense of - wait; what?

Anyway, we still don't know much. We need to fill out forms online for insurance and other stuff - change of mail, for example, phone forwarding, and so on. Sounds like the list is incomplete.

We did get a PO Box:

Dale & Shan Darling

PO Box 7314

Loveland, CO 80537-0314

If you plan to send something, please be precise as the Postal folks are unforgiving in these things. If you have sent something to the old PO, well, we'll see if it is forwarded or not.

Right now, we don't have an address to get anything via other parcel deliveries, so hang on until where we'll be is settled. I suppose we'll need to figure out the transportation issues first - 3 people have offered a vehicle.

I think this is about it for now. Shan has had some emotional moments today, and I think we're both sort of settling a bit. Even though most of the comments we're getting have to do with stuff, there are many that also say that folks are praying for us, asking their congregations to pray. And I know there are prayer warriors out there who have a direct line with Our Father, that He hears and responds according to His Will. (How often we think it should be our will; aren't we a mess?)

Well, I think a few of you will get this, and I hope a few others will seek more as a result. It's interesting how focused one can become during emotional duress or abject terror.

At breakfast, we talked about how interesting, delightful and sometimes odd but always right God has and continues to lead us. Shan talked about James 1 and John 17, which she read yesterday, 2 of her favorite reads in the NT.

On Thursday, during our attempt to keep water out - we placed sandbags, I built deflectors, Shan put out every towel/ blanket we had along doors - we held out optimism that the rising water would stabilize, then drop. Shan thought, "You know, I wanted to replace the carpet in the back room before the kids came last summer, but we couldn't afford it. So I thought, we'll keep the water out of the hall, pull up that ugly, worn out golden stuff and get new!"

She felt we could isolate the damage, but was willing to sacrifice the back room's carpet.

Meanwhile, the water began to seep through the sliding door we use as our main entrance. We kept working. As that water rose, Shan backed towards the room with the piano, said "I'm drawing the line here!" lifted her arms out and started yelling at the water to STAY OUT! (I heard none of this because I was knee deep in water flowing across the deck, trying to figure out how to move it away from that door.) As the water continued rising, she saw that it was not going to stop, and gave it up, then screamed at me, "Dale, get in here - we've got to get out!"

After several hollers - I couldn't hear anything other than the rush of water - she got through and we took Max and got out. (Please read the following for those details.)

This morning, relating this story, Shan said, "I realized that the main reason I wanted the water to stay out of that room had to do with protecting the piano, because there was an important connection with you and the piano. I didn't want to give in." (We bought the piano when Shan insisted we have an excellent piano to play when a doctor said I had a brain tumor; she didn't want me to die before I had something that I'd always hoped for, but never thought was possible to get. As it turned out, I lost the hearing in my right ear, which made playing very painful, then lost the use of my left hand, making playing impossible. Funny old world, huh?)

I walked into the cabin in my waders to collect a few items - the only few we thought we needed, since we still held out hope that the water would stop rising, then drop - and Shan started to cry and sob. "I need to cry," she said. I held her as the water rose around our calves and dropped from her lovely eyes.

Anyway, James says to count it all joy when you are challenged because it builds character and perfects faith in Father. (Read it yourself for the precise quote.) And I said, "You, know, that explains why we're not worked up about the loss of the stuff, and why so many friends and family seem befuddled by our sense of...peace about this." She agreed. We continued.

Shan said, "I realized that the cabin was behind me, it was in the past: finished. And I'm glad I cut my hand, because it is new and my life line from God. He will use it as a reminder that the cabin - our house - is behind us. We can't go back. My new life line is in the future."

She continued, "This is part of me (the cut). This is a monumental thought. The cut is and will remain as a physical reminder."

And then, "I was mesmerized by the power of the water. It changed constantly as things washed away. The whole channel moved; there was a diversion. The flow, its power, was relentless. And I realized God's power was far greater. His love was far beyond. Water can knock things out of the way - God can knock barriers out of the way."

In John 17, Jesus says something about His Father giving Him these people: I want them with Me. As You and I are One, I want them with me.

That's it for now. A helicopter is flying over as I type this. The sound for us, now, is one of great hope and comfort because that sound brought us hope of rescue and relief. Relief is yet to come, but we are neither stressed nor worried. The adventure continues.

Read on for the first day's installment. I'll write more as we know more.

Love to you all,

dale & Shan

In emails people sent us, other tragedies were mentioned. And during the beginning of our new adventure, we knew of other family deaths, health issues, problems with relationships and heard the fear in friends' voices as we talked or shared emails. Shan's friend Damaris was quick to get clothing to both Shan and I; a few days later, she learned that she had breast cancer, and we cried together. (She's still in treatment.) Another friend was challenged by an ongoing problem with her husband, and the behavior of their young son, then got very ill and was laid up for two months while the other stuff kept swirling as in an eddy. We comforted many others along the way, often becoming the comforter for those who were attempting to comfort us: an interesting occurrence.

A PERSPECTIVE

In Eden Adam and Eve knew Life - God - and walked with Him.

But, of their own volition, they ate forbidden fruit from the tree of the knowledge of good and evil. Then, they knew self; knew embarrassment and fear, and were tossed out of the Garden of Eden for punishment and for their own protection. They needed to be protected from eating the acceptable, previously permitted fruit from the Tree of Life. God did not want them to remain eternally expelled from Life, separated from Him, living in sin. Their fallen nature continues to be our lot; everyone is now born dead spiritually, and must be made alive by being born again. That's something that confused Nicodemus, still confuses many, even though Jesus made it clear: *That which is born of the flesh is flesh; that which is born of the spirit is spirit.*

After Thursday, water-rising day, and by sometime on Friday, I recall thinking that all I had left was a story that was unfolding before my eyes. This realization perked up my observation sensors: I watched and listened to Shan and our neighbors to see and hear how they responded to the flood events.

I only knew a few of the neighbors well. The limited knowledge of the rest was due mostly to the fact that this group of people shared little that was meaningful. Most preferred confrontation to familiarity. Still, there were changes in how people interacted, at least temporarily, and a few showed a little openness, but very little.

Within a short time of seeing the damage to the cabin, our home, and being awed by what the water had done, Shan began to weep, and said, "I need to hug the girls." As she said it, she held out her arms in an imaginary embrace. After a moment, I walked into her open arms and said, "For now, we have one another.

This followed her pronouncement of L2, our discussion about the new adventure, about a clean canvas. In that moment - was it a shock of realization? - creating a new life and living its adventure seemed fine. In retrospect, and within a few days of being flown out, the whole L2-clean-canvas thing seemed lost. Again, it might have been the shock of realization, or the realization of shock, but the emotional duress, which took different forms in Shan and me, made us focus on the present. We reverted to forms and set habits. The future was as a dim dream, and still is. So many things are dependent on how other bureaucratic entities decide things will look.

All of it seemed story-worthy. And I knew writing it would be the main relief I'd get because while creating I ruminate and pray.

The forms were born out of habit and style developed during our 57 and 61 trips around the sun, and 35 years of marriage. Habit and style, to a degree, become ingrained, akin to having brown hair or blue eyes, and are where we go when our systems are under strain, when they are fatigued and tested. I see the world from a six-foot-four inch platform, while Shan's is built at five-six. It's a different perspective seeing over or looking down into someone's eyes from seeing into or looking up into same. For example. And then, there is the male-female difference, how we see the world, how we respond to stress and surprise, how we do or don't, will or won't, emote, and how our minds function when overwhelming events occur: some of the most profound surprises live there. Within this line of thinking, the meaning of not being unequally yoked becomes clearer. We are equally yoked, committed to each other. Our relationship began with knowing we both were loved by, and loved, God. We knew He brought us together, designed and raised us to be attracted to one another, to fall in love and to get, then stay, married. How many times that has been made clear through our marriage, through the emotional and physical challenges that so often result in the dissolving of such relationships, in giving up and moving away. Knowing, as we do, that we're together as part of His mystical, loving will for us individually and together, makes quitting a non option. We'll stay married until death parts us.

We both knew that this trial, like others had done, would build character - we still know this, know it's happening over two months into this adventure - but that didn't mean, doesn't mean, that we always embrace the process of such an increase. (As I typed this, Shan walked into the farm house weeping. She carried a red vest that she found in the few items we kept after my dad died in 2003, and said, "I think this was your dad's Indian Guide vest from when you were little, and it's covered in mold." And then, "I don't know why I feel like this." I let her cry it out, and answered her question with, "Sure; go ahead and throw it away if it can't be cleaned." I felt sad at the flicker of memory of a little boy - I was the boy - and his dad, together. She weeps because she's an emotional, compassionate woman with a singular imagination; it's part of her style, part of her charm.)

Early on after our rescue, Shan acknowledged that her mind was not working in a clear manner. But when I asked her to trust me while explaining that mine was working, was thinking clearly, she responded in a manner other than I had hoped she would. She became defensive, and got a little angry. Shan's confusion, and the impatience it initiates, continued, continues still, as she heals, while she deals with the emotional angst she knows. (The tears at dad's vest are a relief from this; I think they clear some of the stress.) Shan has been able to focus on the thing at hand, has performed well at work, on organizing the farm house into a home - an ongoing project - while going through the cabin, cleaning and making decisions, one thing at a time. Healed emotions will take longer.

Habits are ingrained by practice and discipline either of the flesh or in the Spirit. *Of the world* is the style we have established from habit, good and bad. *In* but not *of the world*, comes by faith: hearing and responding to God's initiative through His Word, by Grace.

Through the years, I've come to realize - believe? - certain basic tenets. They include:

Truth and time go hand in hand. Jesus is Truth.

Courage is character on display.

Character - perfection - comes from trials, as does patience.

Patience is the first requirement to learn or to teach anything.

Character, or its lack, like patience and strength, are activated in - or by - adversity, and grow during adversity's reign. I admit that the flood has tested us in its aftermath, and continues to do so. But I keep *truth and time go hand in hand*, and the *building of character and patience* near for perspective.

And then I ask, *In light of what I know* (how I am known?) *how shall I live?*

Does God, through Holy Spirit, allow us glimpses through the mirror in which we dimly see? A view past the fog of poor focus, into both, or either, the micro of a day or the perspective of a thousand years? I wonder.

Do we miss hearing for the noise? I think so. *Father, calm my heart and lower the volume of selfish noise; let your voice come clear, like the trumpet that cuts through the rumble of battle and sounds victory.*

Jesus Is Peace. His Peace He left us, we who are grafted into the I Am.

On Tuesday, September 17th, the third day off the mountain, I wrote this e-mail to continue informing family and friends, and to answer questions of a similar nature that we received.

Hi,

It's the flooded out pests once again!

Shan and I have been talking again this morning about a variety of things. It's very interesting. One of the topics has to do with the generous offers many of you have made. Honestly, I have not been able to keep track of them, so we decided to send this note as a specific response.

If you've made a specific offer of housing, thank you, but until we hear from FEMA we're up in the air. We hope to hear today, and based on what we heard yesterday, think there is a good chance that this will occur. I'll let you know.

Several have offered a vehicle, as well. Thanks. So far, the answer is the same. We do have 2 cars that in theory are safe in Drake, but Drake will be inaccessible for several months, I think. There's a chance that our insurance will pay for a car, but I don't know how long that will take. For now, we're imposing on Jessica and working out getting around. Being an imposition is an interesting thing just now. You'll need to wait for the book that is percolating in my head for thoughtful, honest details.

Others have made offers that are either specific to an item - clothes, shoes, a Kindle, etc - or more vague, as in, "How can I help?"

Someone suggested gift cards - two folks who did so thought about Home Depot, but there's nothing to repair as we have no house; kind as the thought is - a great first place to go - I don't think we need any home improvement items just now.

As Shan and I talked, she thought Visa cards would work because we can use them for food, gas, clothing and gasoline. Then she said that she thought they cost the giver extra. Honestly, I have no idea how they work. I know Shan loves JC Penny's and there is a store in Ft. Collins that we could use. As far as I can tell, it's still open.

If anyone wants to send a check, that will also work. If you'd prefer to wait until we know more, that would also be just fine.

Our new address is

PO Box 7314

Loveland, CO 80537

We're very low on cell phone minutes, but I guess texting is unlimited. If you'd like to call or text, please text to Shan only - I'm handling emails - or call either of us as needed.

I'm not comfortable writing this, but love each of you who have offered help and assistance. If your head is clearer than mine, which would not be very hard, do what makes sense to you at this time, or wait until later, or until you forget and everything passes. Funny how that sort of thing works out, isn't it?

To my fly tying friends who have offered tying tools and materials - Russell and others, forward this as you will - please just wait. I now think that as soon as we find a place, I'll want to tie some flies in order to sort out my thoughts and emotions. So far, writing these notes is all that I have along that line, instead using energy to help Shan and the girls, others who need to vent, and so on. There will be no music for me, so the tying - and writing - will sort of be it.

THANKS!!!! to all of you from the depths of our beings. Thanks for caring, for being out there, for your thoughtful prayers made in obedience and according to God's will.

I'll continue to send reports. Forward this to whomever you'd like.

With love and humility

dale & Shan Darling

And, as was the case for the time being, comments and emails poured in. This came from Brittany's husband, one of my two sons.

Thanks for the update, Dale. I've had emails from people all over the country wanting to know how my family is doing. One of the leaders in our church approached me today to ask how the church can support you. He said once things settle a little bit and you figure out what's going on and where to go from here, to let him know and he'll organize something. I imagine it would be best to send money, that way you can use it for your most urgent needs. You should be getting a package from us tomorrow. I put a few moleskines in there. Maybe you can sketch out your book in there. I don't know what avenue you're considering for publishing, but I've made friends with a literary agent who may be interested. Again, if you decide to leave beautiful Colorado, our home is open. We can move the dogs from the room with the fire place and you guys can take that over. It's not as pretty here, but relatively calm and peaceful, plus the seminary library is close by. And a few coffee shops. Talk to you soon. Do you need books?

Love,

Russ

On Tuesday after our evacuation, Don came to the valley to retrieve his Bobcat, which had been repaired. Because the highways from Estes to Loveland, Lyons and Boulder were closed, he had to drive south from Estes Park to Highway 6 near Black Hawk, east to Golden, and then to his daughter's house in north Denver. The normal seventy-five minute drive to the valley took almost four hours! After spending the night with Andrea, her husband and their two young children, Don headed north and stopped to see Shan and I at the Coffee Tree. He gave us loving support, filled us in on what he'd been doing in Estes, and gave us a generous check. His gift allowed us a modest sigh of relief, and made Shan cry. After, he drove east to Greeley, then made the long haul back to Estes. When we talked later that evening, he told me some of the roads south of Estes were undermined by floodwater, but quick repairs allowed heavy truck traffic that hauled fuel, food and supplies to Estes Park. (Other towns had been completely cut off by the flood.) Soon, the road would carry very heavy equipment and road crews to operate it in their quest to reconstruct and

Don, my brother, and me

repair Highway 34 from Estes Park to Loveland, Highway 36 from Estes Park to Lyons, and Highway 119 from Boulder to Nederland. Before a federal government shutdown closed it, crews traveled Trail Ridge Road through Rocky Mountain National Park to deliver enormous construction equipment where it was needed along the northern front range.

On Saturday, after Don had made an introduction with his friend Craig, and we'd gotten moved to the farm - one week after we were evacuated from Drake - Shan and I met Don in Longmont and ate a meal together at Mike O'Shay's, as good a pub as I know. He filled us in further on what was going on in Estes, what he was hearing, both fact and speculation, and when Larraine, his wife, might be able to return from her trip to Ohio.

Don was to have left to fly to Ohio on water-rising day. He'd asked me to drive him to Denver International Airport (DIA), which became moot when he couldn't get out of Estes, and Highway 34 from Drake was closed. The fact that he missed his flight became a blessing to his Estes neighbors, but much more to me. The repaired Bobcat was used to good purpose when he moved trees, assisted friends, and opened thoroughfares so people could get out and about. The city authorities asked and Don made inspections of commercial buildings, which expedited owners' ability to clean up and reopen their businesses to serve their neighbors. Don said he had 2-1/2 hours of emails to answer every night, which is frustrating for him. My brother doesn't like to type all that much, but is an excellent extemporaneous speaker: he spins a tight yarn. Don was exhausted and alone. But he persevered, kept going, cleaned water damage to the home where he and Larraine live, as well as to other property they own, while encouraging and helping his community. It's what leaders do.

Larraine drove back to Colorado with their son, Adam, two weeks after the flood. Before they returned, arrangements were made, and once the Volvo was back, we worked out the details to borrow the car; it was another of Don's and Larraine's generous, tangible help. Adam helped Don, and got to visit his Colorado sisters, brother-in-law, niece and nephew for a few days before flying back to Ohio and the heart of his own young family.

In addition to all of that, Don's eighty-eight-year-old friend, Dennis, was dying of pancreatic cancer; Don visited him every day. Dennis' nieces, 69 and 56, his only living relatives, were with him, too. (Each of their husbands had died of cancer.) Just a week before the flood hit, Don drove all of them to a very special celebration in Iowa that Dennis really wanted to attend. Don and the girls weren't sure he'd live until the event, let alone survive the trip. But he did, and thoroughly enjoyed the ceremony honoring his ancestors. After returning to Estes Park, Dennis went to a nursing home with hospice care; Don was with Dennis when he died. It was all hard on Don; but he endured, persevered and did many kindnesses for Dennis, his nieces and many others.

Dennis died on September 25. Don was with him, talking to him about how much their friendship meant, and so on. When Don and I visited later that day - he was alone in Estes, pretty isolated and very busy - he said, "I realized that Dennis' temple was no longer fit for him to live in. His spirit departed as I held his hand, and I knew he was free." We talked about the mixed emotions - Dennis was 89, his body was full of cancer, and he had lost his wife of over 60 years a few years earlier; they didn't have children. Don was one of his few friends in the area. It was his time; the man lived a good, full life, loved God and knew that he was loved. Regardless, Don would miss his friend.

I hope the bears and raccoons are feasting on the food that was in the fridge.

I wonder about the trout, aquatic insects, trees, and other trout stream denizens; know that grass, flowers and streamside vegetation were gone.

*O*ur stuff is mostly ruined, but here I sit with a laptop, cell phone and Kindle, and electricity to operate all of it. Not quite like having to brave the mule cart being washed away with no hope for a replacement, for any outside help, is it?

We received lots of help; it came in fast! Most was from friends and family members, while other forms of help came from different sources. Of course a few were surprising.

When FEMA insisted that we provide receipts for Shan's visit to the emergency stitchery, she finally called the place to get an official bill. While we'd filled out change of address forms online, had received mail at our forwarding address in Loveland, and so on, nothing had come from the urgent care center. After the call, Shan came to me in tears.

"I kept asking for the records, the woman asked for more and more specific information, and eventually called on a supervisor. She came back, and said 'We can't find any bill for your visit; there is no bill to be paid.'" Someone had helped us in a generous, anonymous manner. (I wonder if it was our angel RN.)

We heard from people we didn't know. *You don't know us, but our congregation is praying for you.* Others sent money, gifts, and so on. People forwarded emails; friends of friends dropped us lines of concern or encouragement. We shook our heads and counted our blessings, gave thanks, and continued, one day at a time, to do the next thing. We did what we could do, one thing at a time.

On the other hand, as it turns out, bureaucracies and many people - we're getting massive doses of each - often behave in similar nefarious manners. They function by well designed forces of habit and rules that define function and comfort level, and result in predetermined conclusions that are in their favor.

We also experienced good intentions that, once acted upon, were altered after the fact. What happens? Perhaps a rush - an emotional gush - of inspiration to help, to respond, is replaced by a person's normal emotions that define their comfort zone, a comfort zone that doesn't actually allow for action based on good intent. Words are easy to say. Don thinks the expression/statement, *Our thoughts and prayers are with you,* is the beginning, middle and end of that whole thing. Even though initial intentions were kind, their withdrawal caused us grief and more unsettledness. While that wasn't something we needed at the time, I continued to realize that it was important to comfort - at times by leaving alone - people we encountered who made, then withdrew offers of help. It was, as I said, difficult. Also, as one door shut another opened; we pressed on, day by day, event to event, one thing at a time.

Representatives of our insurance company, FEMA, The Red Cross, and so on, at least in our initial conversations, respond when they call us, or when we see or call them, like this: "I'm so sorry about this. How can we help?" But that's before rules, regulations and guidelines stipulate what will happen - or what won't. As conversations unfolded, I've said, "So there is no help; nothing that you'll do." And they've said, "I'm so sorry for your loss." But that's before they get angry, and say, "I'm only trying to do my job." Or, "I have a job to do." And, like I said, similar things happened with individuals we thought were friends, too.

A person who answered the phone at The Red Cross said, "We have shelters, food and resources."

I asked, "What resources?"

"Shelters, food and resources to help."

"What resources to help?"

"Insurance company contact numbers..."

!!!!

"Thanks," I say, "I wish you the best." Then, I hang up. I knew how to reach our insurance agent, who, along with other representatives of that company, expanded my previous description by being aloof, flippant or just unhelpful, depending on the moment's mood.

In these cases - it became the norm - I must provide comfort to the one who thinks they are the comforter, one in the position to be the comforter. Obviously, the flood's aftermath has been hard on a lot of people, including those pressed into service who should provide comfort. Many, like Shan and I, are out of their element. I think many are overwhelmed. I hope a few develop character in response to the challenges.

Early on, but after a few of these transactions, Shan decided that we shouldn't stay with or borrow things from friends or acquaintances, due to the flip-flop changes of heart we experienced. Such a line of thinking is difficult for us to accept, because the flip-flops surprised us, maybe more than the obvious rising water and what its relentless flow accomplished. It created a dilemma of curious proportions, eh? But there was the other hand, too.

For example, an ill friend with an uncooperative husband and troubled-by-his-behavior young son (the young son's behavior, you see) wanted to help us, as did her parents. She needed rest and a return to hearty health, and time with her son. Still, she encouraged us and insisted we call her folks and accept their help.

A PLACE TO STAY

We did find a good spot to live - we're still there, as I edit this these few days before Christmas 2013 - and again in early April 2014! The stability of place has tremendous value in a situation like ours. (Even so, we continue to know we are unsettled and feel vulnerable.)

On September 20, I sent out the next mass e-mail, informing family and friends of a new development.

Hello again!

First, thanks to each of you for your prayers and physical support. Today we received a few checks and other donations which we really appreciate. Thanks. Also, we continue to get emails that are encouraging and full of hope. Thanks.

This morning we confirmed that we have a place to stay for the foreseeable future. In other words an open ended invite from people we don't know, but will. My brother, Don, who lives in Estes Park, was telling a friend of his what was up with us, and the man said they had a place. I'll post a few pix tomorrow. It is small and does not have a kitchen, but Shan is certain it will work out. One of the best things is that it's in the country, out of city lights - one of the things we loved about out streamside home was the dark at night, the quiet at most times. When I walked in, my first observation was "What a good place to write!" I plan to start writing a book about this event; guess we'll see if I have it or not.

Shan and Jessica at the farm Brittany said "Who knew it came stocked with cute blonds?"

By early afternoon we'd moved the few meager items we have. Tonight, Max, the chowderhead golden retriever, will be back with us. Shan is presently at a disaster relief meeting that's supposed to be covering logistics and plans for roads and so on. I just don't have the energy for that just now.

This afternoon, Shan went to Jess' new apartment to help her clean and get settled; I took a brief nap in the new place. My deep slumber was disturbed by a phone call from FEMA - to our overseas friends, this is a US federal agency that responds when the president says a natural event creates a disaster area, which happened here last week. The representative was an info taker who wanted to verify that we were displaced, owned and lived in the property. (I'd called to answer a set of questions on Monday.) She said we'd hear something within a few days in the form of some money for temporary relief. That when access to the house is available, someone from FEMA would come to examine the damage, which you've already seen in the pix I posted. We may face some challenges because we didn't have flood insurance. When we bought the place in 2001 we were told it was not required because we weren't in the flood plain. Go figure.

We saw a neighbor from up the mountain from us who said there was looting going on up there. Since there was no way to lock up, the front of the cabin blown out and all, there will be a possibility that some of what's up there may not be there when we can get access to it. Oh well.

I was also thinking that since the fridge had been forced into the front area that was destroyed, and that it was open, chances are good that a bear and perhaps a few raccoons will be feasting. It would be good that something got something out if this, right?

Shan's doing well, and sends her love. She plans to return to work on Tuesday, which means I'll remove half of the stitches - advise from a medical friend - on Monday. Her hand is healing well, and we're pleased that she's experienced little pain.

So, that's it for now.

Thanks again for the ongoing support! More as the drama continues to unfold.

Love,

dale & Shan

The time finally comes, when our ill, unsettled dear friend calls to invite us to dinner. It's a work night for Shan, but so far all we've done is eat out. (The one time we tried eating in caused all sorts of emotional distress for the fellow we were staying with, and forced us to find a new place much sooner than we'd wanted to; then, the new place has worked great, and the owners have been generous in many ways.)

When we arrived - after Shan returned from work and changed, she said *let's go!* - our friend introduced us to her folks and her 21-year-old daughter. We'd met her 10-year-old son when he and his mom visited the cabin. He was playing with toys - a good thing for a young boy to do. Everyone was kind and gracious. We both relaxed a little. A baseball playoff game was on the TV. We talked about what was going on. Dad had specific questions;

mom was quiet, observant and available for any need. We had tea; the meal was ready.

Dad served Shan, who cried with joy at this simple expression of hospitality. The dinner and conversation were dandy, free and full. No strings attached: we felt loved and accepted. Their clear, sincere expression was needed, and appreciated. It was good: warm, like a scarf on our cold necks.

That evening, Shan experienced another touch of tenderness when our friend's son left his seat at the table, walked to where Shan sat and, with a child's intuition that told him he needed to act, gave Shan a long, gentle, comforting hug. Then, as a memento of the moment, he handed Shan a special rock from his collection. (Jessica always collected rocks at that age, and still has a box full.) Shan has this talisman and, like her scar, uses it to recall L2 - Life Two, post-flood.

For many years, I've thought that people have different propensities and capacities that come preloaded by God: Creator, Sustainer and Future. Each person has the capacity to hear and to receive, as well as individual will - volition - to listen and accept that which God offers. Or not. And I think we know when we don't listen and reject.

In early October, as we received more info, I sent this update. Responses had begun to wane. I think most people were finished with this particular disaster, but I still wanted to keep folks in the loop. I suppose there were many cases of *What more can I say?* Which was fair enough!

Hi.

I hope this finds everyone who reads doing well. For the most part it sounds like folks are back in gear, doing normal stuff and moving on. And that seems just fine, all things taken together.

Shan worked all week this week - Monday-Thursday, her usual week - and really did pretty well. Her hand is healing very well, but causes a little irritation when she closes it and her ring finger nail pokes at the incision. She's wearing a bandage over it, and none of the issues - nail poking or healing wound - has kept her from doing the things she wants to do.

My brother, Don, went to a meeting in Estes last night. Road repair - specifically 34 from Loveland to Estes, thus passing through Drake - was the topic, and the fellow leading it said they have a rough road - called a pioneer road - through from Estes to Drake already. They will open it to 4-wheel drive vehicles on Sunday from noon-5 p.m., and are working from dawn to dusk every day in both directions. Apparently there are 50 large pieces of equipment, more on the way, on both ends of the Narrows, working towards one another. They are confident that will be open - maybe one lane gravel - by December 1, safe and passable. Also, they said that 119 from Boulder to Nederland will open within about 2 weeks. That will make the trip from this area to Estes 2 hours shorter each way - a big help for residents, businesses, deliveries and workers.

So there you have it. Shan and my friend Dave Moore are champing at the bit to get up there. While that now would be possible - Don would drive them down to Drake in his truck - I've said no for now because they won't be able to get to the cabin - the river is too fast and deep - and there is no reason to check on the cars because we wouldn't be able to drive them out, anyway. The flow out of the dam in Estes is 244 cfs, which is higher than I like to wade or fish the river. Since it is no longer in its established streambed, I assume the bed is unstable and challenging to wade. I think that CDOT will install a temporary bridge as soon as possible somewhere near the cabin so they can access the buildings on our street. We heard that they'll use Army bridges until decisions for permanent ones are made, then built.

Many family's homes are isolated by the river because smaller, lighter bridges were destroyed by high water pushing debris - often bits of other homes washed away, huge trees, vehicles and anything else you can imagine:

okay, probably no space ships. It sounds like thing one is build a road that is passable from one end to the other; thing 2 will be bridges, and then the process of assessing damage, deciding areas that will be condemned or fixed, starting the repairs to smaller bridges and homes, then really fixing the roads, paving and so on.

This morning, I read that Colorado's governor is suggesting that the very expensive road repairs made after the 1976 flood that were suppose to withstand a 500 year flood - that's what they are calling our flood - failed, and perhaps the road should be less expensive but practical so it won't cost so much to replace it in another 20-30 years when this happens again. Sounds like good thinking to me.

I wonder what decisions will be made on the river. In Colorado, rivers that run through the mountains are mostly considered irrigation ditches, vessels to move water that will irrigate grass, and agricultural lands. If wildlife can live there, fine, but don't let any of it get in the way of water movement, traffic travel or anything else that is more important. It would seem that the last lesson, similar to the road construction that occurred post-1976, concerning the river, which was artificially deepened and moved to accommodate the important stuff, were not learned. Note, the artificial bed that was dug through our area following the '76 flood was filled with boulders, rocks and sand during the flood, and went where it wanted to go. Right now, it looks like a wild river, flowing free.

Interesting.

Well, that's a short update. Hope it's useful and that you're well.

Thanks again for your support, encouragement, prayers and donations. It's good to see Shan back on her feet, thriving in helping patients while working with her great boss and the staff he's assembled.

Love, dale

MORE PERSPECTIVE

Because something isn't my fault doesn't necessarily make it someone else's fault, right?

It's a common trait of fallen humanity to fault another, to shift and negotiate blame. After eating the fruit from the tree of the knowledge of good and evil and being confronted by God, Adam said, "The woman you gave me," made me eat it, thus faulting his Maker and his wife in one breath. (Husbands continue this trend.) Eve blamed the serpent. Flip Wilson's *The devil made me do it!* got laughs of agreement on Laugh In, and the first Adam's progeny continue to place fault.

And to demand recompense. We're seeing this now as people want to find blame and file lawsuits.

Fallen, sinful man is a common enough set of terms, at least in the West, where over thousands of years the story of redemption has been taught, written about and shared. The Fall was the result of Adam disobeying God, eating the fruit. But what happened? Well, all humans born ever after are not fully human; we are born spiritually dead, incomplete. God made Adam completely human, to live forever in His presence. Adam's choice to do as he pleased was possible because God created him with free will to do as he pleased. He chose poorly. Adam was tossed out of Eden, had to earn his keep by the sweat of his brow, and eventually died physically, as well as spiritually.

Jesus came to redeem all of humanity, to make a person fully human again. I think that's what we long for: to be complete. Sadly, keeping score and blaming others for faults of our own - or a flood - sidetracks us from Truth.

In the 1970s Francis Schaeffer wrote a book and made a film series that was called, How Shall We Then Live? I read the book and watched the films, which focused on art - music, painting, architecture, sculpture - as it made manifest man's interpretation of God's Creation. Man, made by God in His Image, is creative and creates.

For years, as I read Scripture, I found myself asking of specific, meaningful verses, *So, is that true or not true?* As difficult as it often seemed, because of what the passage said, what it indicated I might do, or what it meant about what someone had said, I always answered, *Yes.*

As a result, I came to ask myself, *In light of what I now know, how shall I then live?*

Well, the Light, Who casts out darkness and illuminates His Way, is bright and casts no shadows because He is everywhere and timeless. He is life. As far as I can tell, limited as I am and all, that is so.

It appears that Truth - Life - Is beyond the tyranny of the immediate as I experience it. Tyranny is based on circumstances that impose themselves on the flesh I inhabit and cause pain I feel and also see in others; in noise I hear, and odors that taste of death. This beyond-the-tyranny vision, God's gift, brings perspective learned from hind sight - life, so far, does go on - that results in trust, the knowledge and understanding that Jesus bears burdens to make a light yoke, and that often, I am the burden He bears.

Along the way, I have become aware of tactile pain, grief, and the emotional outbursts they activate, and realize these, in fact, are not reality, but are temporary even though the events leave scars. Reality, for me as a Christian saved by God's grace through the working of the power of the strength of His might, is found in the position where He put me, which is seated in Christ at the right hand of the Father. In Life, rather than in death. Life is reality.

T oday - it's a month tomorrow since we fled the rising water - I'm not as likely to hear and feel the sound and the wet of the rain, the roar and the vibration of the flood of water, or smell the lingering scent of ruin. That's a change. It makes sense that time heals. After three days of the sound of rushing water and of feeling the rumble of tumbling boulders' vibrations through every part of my body, the echo remained and is still there, but it's dimmer. While the sound fades, my emotional response is still working its way through my system. (It's over a month since I wrote that before typing this, and last night I had another everything-is-getting-wet-because-the-water-is-rising dream.)

I know this is the case with Shan, and from what I hear and observe in her, it's still pretty loud. Last night, she said she realized that work is taking all of her mental energy, and that it comes from a different part of her brain - I think it's the trained part, the part that can allow work by rote to happen. At the conclusion of the workday, she said she was aware of empty exhaustion, and of the need to cry. We continue to receive notes, cards and gifts, and each one allows Shan another opportunity to cry for a few moments while she also considers how many people our dilemma has affected, and how they have responded in love. For Shan, crying has always been both an emotional response and a form of relief. I'm glad she cries; that she can and will.

Tonight, after work, Shan is going to meet our friend, Roberta, who has collected some tools for us. Basic tools mean a lot to Shan. When she graduated from high school, her dad gave her a small, blue, molded plastic tool box that was stuffed with practical odds and ends. (He did the same for each of our daughters.) Shan kept it with her all through college and brought it into our marriage. It's possible that the little blue tool box is still in the garage, but we won't know until Don can haul his Bobcat - we call it Bob - to the cabin and clear away the concrete-hard sand that blocks the garage door. And we'll have to cut up tree trunks, move our own and others' debris before Bob can get to that sand. It'll be long, hard work.

As it turns out, it takes a lot of people, their skills and talents, to make a recovery, to sort through debris, to assess needs and to fill them. And it looks like our part is to sort through the internal mess. In fact, we can't do the physical sorting without letting family, friends and other generous people do most of it, and we can't do the internal work at all, other than by realizing that it is a *Thy will be done*, not a *my will be done* operation. His will is done by Him when we trust and obey.

I'm struck by the Jesus-is-the-Shepherd-and-we-are-the-sheep thingy. *The sheep Know My voice*, He says, *and follow me*. The sheep go along in the flock, as long as they are healthy. When one falters, He carries it. The other sheep must notice in their sheepish way.

The lamb being carried also has a different view than the moving, grazing flock has: they only see other sheep butts. And the air is fresher up here, cradled in the arms or thrown over the shoulders of the Shepherd. Here, there is rest in the midst of the trial. Here, there is relief; there is hope; there is a view!

In the midst of various trials, others take note of how the tried one responds. Do they know when the tried one is being carried by Jesus? That when one responds by faith, by His gift and according to His initiative, Truth and Life are expressed and made known?

"My yoke is easy, my burden is light." It's because He does the work, all for our freedom and His glory.

VARIOUS THOUGHTS

Love thy neighbor as thyself follows *you shall love the Lord your God with all....*

Mostly, it's a good idea to get info and then base behavior - including our thought life - on proper perspective. For years, I've tried to look at the get perspective statement through this: *Truth and time go hand in hand.* And I've looked at truth through the statement that *Jesus is Truth.* (Fact is not truth.) He is also no longer confined by time. But I am so confined. The past and present are fading or clear, and the future soon becomes the present, but by the time I write or think *present* it is past, and the past slides ever further away. Captured in space and time in a body that carries me around and causes all sorts of distractions both evil and good, sad and joyful, I seek to know as I am known by the Timeless.

Who says to love Him with all, and to love my neighbor as myself.

While humans really like to quantify by categories, taking one thing, and splitting it into pieces or adding it to others - and I tend to this style at times - it seems to me that the love Him-neighbor-self is a unity of One, because my neighbor and myself as Christians, are of the I Am. (Loving neighbor is not based on that person's belief or behavior.) The Christian lives in love. God is love, and we're made to know God and to enjoy Him forever. It's a timeless forever. Still, time is something humans enjoy quantifying and categorizing. That and the weather. (We complain about both.)

Quantifying and categorizing are two of many ways humans use to be partial about this or about that. Certain partiality is a matter of style: we like a particular food more than another, for example. But toward our neighbor, whom we are to love as we love ourselves, there should be no partiality. As it turns out, there is partiality because we are so partial to ourselves.

When a disaster such as our flood occurs, it makes others, temporarily, more partial to us.

Recently, it dawned on me - it's interesting how God, at the right time for us, and for others, illuminates the particulars we mull over - that the behavior Adam and Eve first manifested after eating fruit from the tree of the knowledge of good and evil had to do with knowledge of themselves: of self, of I. Before eating the forbidden fruit,

127

their world was with God. They must have been aware of Life, of being complete and perfect: alive. When they ate the fruit, they became aware of themselves, and hid in fear to protect self. Later, when confronted by God, they blamed God, one another, and the serpent.

Ever since The Fall, people live as though the world revolves around them. This makes me think that the *love myself* should not be self love, like the self infatuation that we know and observe in ourselves and in others, but is something else. And *love thy neighbor* is not done in order to build up thy self, not to accumulate more self love.

W hat is our perspective on time? Earlier, I wrote, *Jesus is no longer confined by time*. (It's because He created time for us.) But I am so confined. When God, the Son Jesus, became human, He was confined by time, as we are. But, He was also the first complete human since before Adam sinned and was tossed out of paradise - the presence of God - and human Jesus didn't sin, was sacrificed, killed dead, for the sin of the world, then made alive to make Man completely human, and full of Life, abundant Life. He did without sin what other men did in sin.

B eing partial to something brings focus on that for which we are partial. When it's self, self love and care, we focus on self more and more, thus less and less on loving God and others. This focus, then, splits and thus categorizes into parts what is the oneness of love the Lord your God with all, and your neighbor as yourself.

God loves without partiality. It rains on the good and the evil - it floods both, too - and Jesus died, was buried, resurrected, ascended and is seated at the right hand of God to make every human completely human, to make them all whole. Without partiality. Not by works, not by something a person could do to earn this wholeness, but by His grace.

Is being rational seeing and thinking about things as they really are, from an eternal perspective?

One who is irrationally partial to self and stuff would be harder hit by the loss of their stuff, feeling loss to self, as though they'd lost their life, I suppose. At least people who weren't in, but commented on, the flood said things like that to me.

Within us, there is this pot of active emotions, and a supply of inert, yet to be activated emotions. Both must be controlled by intellectual will: how active emotions will influence behavior, and when the inactive will be unleashed.

The challenges Shan and I faced continued. We were bombarded with questions we couldn't answer. People asking the questions who cared, or only wanted to show us how smart they were, often responded with angry exclamations at the answers we forwarded to them. *How can they say that!?* or *That's not fair!* were common responses that felt like attacks on us. We were vulnerable, unsettled and, even in the midst of those who cared, lonely. As it turns out, being a refugee is lonely business.

We wondered where all of the reported help and assistance were going; we weren't getting any of it. We continued doing what we could do, one thing at a time, while wondering what came next. As much as we hoped for answers, I knew our patience and perseverance would be tested and required in order to endure. As it turned out, the big question *When can we get back to the cabin* was answered in early October.

Friday morning, water starts to fall; side door broken, water rushes into the living room
October visit; dry; raccoons and squirrels had cleared the counters; bears came later, ripped doors off cabinets

Friday morning; neighbor's house is gone; front of ours blown out
Water continues to roar through Drake
The Manhole as we saw it on our first trip back
The small hope we had to recover books and so on were dashed

Shan sews on a summer day in her special room
She lovingly crafted quilts, curtains, blankets, pillows and so on
A surge of water - the water line in the back room was seven feet
high - drenched materials; destroyed her machines

In August 2013, Shan and I celebrated our
35th wedding anniversary by planting new flowers
In October 2013, the dirt, flowers, propane tank, road, trees,
fence and so on were all gone

Looking upstream towards our bridge
This area teemed with life! Riparian habitat, where river meets
banks and surrounding land, always does

The drive down the canyon from Estes to Drake
Road, river, riparian habitat: all ruined

RETURNS

It's Sunday, October 13, 2013, just a day past one month since the flood on September 12. Shan borrows a '99 Suburban from a friend's boyfriend, who wants to help: *Borrow my car to move things!*

Jessica and Blake, her boyfriend, join us.

We leave the farm at 7:30 a.m., thirty minutes later than planned, drive southwest to 119, west through Boulder, up Boulder Canyon - it was repaired and opened first, which shortened the trip - to Nederland, and then north on 72, to 7, before arriving in Estes Park (EP). It takes 2 hours.

We go to Don's, pick him up and then go to breakfast in EP. Jess says *It's a breakfast to remember* because she likes it so much. The food was good!

Before ordering, Shan puts clothes into washing machines at a nearby laundromat. When we finish eating, we drive back to Don's and, while everyone else takes a nap - they won't let us down the canyon until noon - Shan goes back to finish drying the clean clothes. At noon, we leave Don's, get gas in a can - in case someone has siphoned gas out of our cars - and drive to Drake. Our optimism remains. Along the way, we are awed by the damage left in the wake of the flood's now receded water.

At Drake: "Let's see if the cars will start," Don says. "They are most important." He's right. We look: both cars are wet inside, and ruined. The optimism we had wanes: no cars. We pictured ourselves driving them out, had decided on the way down that, even though the road is rough, we could do so. Little does that matter now. When we get back in the truck, I see a group of people standing in front of the Stage Stop Inn. They form a circle, join hands, bow their heads in prayer. For many, prayer is all that's left. In worldly man's eyes this seems silly. Often, I think that when we find ourselves - singularly or as a group - devoid of frills, absent what is normal, God has us where we might choose to listen, where we might realize that to trust and obey is the only way to be free. He is always here.

To the cabin: Don drives his big dually diesel truck over the bridge. When we'd been flown out, we knew both approaches to the bridge were gone, but that the bridge was still there. We also knew the streambed had shifted through our front yard, and that the original bed was filled with debris. The material used to fill the washed-out approaches seemed surreal, like gravel, stones and sand that were from a foreign planet; it looked strange - we saw that the workers had dug a new streambed that was deeper and narrower, but mostly followed the original one. (This is a mistake, done out of expediency.) A large water-filled crater remained where our yard had been. The new River Fork Road was

Water condensation on inside of the Nissan: ruined!

136

In the midst of destruction, hands joined in prayer
Shall we build character, or whine? Choose well

narrow, built out of the same material used to repair the bridge approaches. Huge boulders, large rocks and other debris were scattered about the area; piles of other foreign-planet-fill material was everywhere.

Don, Jess and Blake get their first look at the destruction. Shan and I see that there is more damage since we left. Girls go inside and work on filling a few plastic tubs with items on a list Shan made, and with other stuff she thought we could salvage. They select things that were high and dry, that missed getting wet and soiled with mud, sewage and other toxins. It smells bad everywhere. Heavy trucks turn around at Drake; Colorado Department Of Transportation (CDOT) employees seem to linger or loiter, but they could be on a break; flaggers direct the flow of traffic on the now gravel 34 on the other side of the bridge, in front of the still praying folks gathered at the Inn.

Don and Blake grab shovels and try to dig an opening that will allow us to open the garage door. It's supposed to slide, but won't: there is too much gravel, sand and wet mud. Don's back hurts; I don't even try, knowing better. Don breaks slats out of the door with a hammer. We find the inside worse than we'd expected, but still retain hope for the manhole. (When Shan and I moved up here full time, Don built the little room inside the garage so I could work, tie flies and so on. Brittany, our middle daughter, christened it the manhole; the name stuck.) We can't see through the manhole door's window due to the condensation on the inside of it.

It's very muddy in the garage. Blake opens a large plastic tub that stores lots of tying materials; it's full of water, the contents wet and muddy. We don't open any others. Don breaks out the window in the manhole's door: there is way too much mud on both sides of the aluminum door to open it. The manhole is much worse than we expect; our last remnant of hope is dashed. The room is full of wet, stinking mud, and everything has been tossed about by water that was, based on the lines on the walls, at least 5 feet deep, and powerful enough to upend both big, solid oak bookcases full of my books. Sad day.

We get a few things out, then leave the manhole and garage. Everything we save will need to be cleaned and repaired. Blake finds the pair of ski poles he bought Jessica for her birthday, and is glad. There is no sign of her new skis; we see it, but her snowboard is buried too deep in mud to get it out. Later, we realize there were actually two boards. One was completely covered in wet, stinky mud.

Don and Blake put their backs to the test: trying to move heavy, wet, congealed mud away from the garage door

The girls have also done enough; we load the truck, get in and drive back to Don's. The mood is low; it gets lower as we drive away and on up the canyon. (The driving that day took much longer than the amount of time we spent at the cabin.)

After arriving at Don's, unloading his truck, and putting boxes of salvaged stuff in the borrowed Suburban, we order pizza, drink a beer and watch the end of the Broncos' game on TV. We leave Don at 6:04 p.m., gloomy, fatigued and low. The drive back to the farm is long and dark: it mimes our mood, which is gloomy and gets worse with each mile. Everyone is quiet. (Later, Shan notes it was though a dark cloud hung over us, followed us and made us feel darker.) There is a lot of traffic, others heading south on the Peak to Peak Highway to Nederland. Shan sleeps; Jess naps. I stop in Nederland to buy a soda, sip it to calm my stomach - always a problem organ after pizza. After the long drive down Boulder Canyon, through that city and northeast to and through Longmont, we arrive at the farm, our new home, at 8:40 p.m., tired.

Max is glad to see us, and expresses dog delight in spite of our mood, which he lifts.

We unload the Suburban, leave particularly muddy items, in other words almost everything we salvaged, outside. Jess and Shan, Blake and I form and share a circle hug, and Shan cries softly, then with more vigor when I tell her to let it go. Jess' tears join Shan's - a good thing. I'm glad the girls express their emotions, that they have this release of tears. I wish I could cry, or would. The kids leave.

I take a shower to wash away the stink and something else, then write the outline of this report. I hope to sleep.

Slept; woke. Before rising, Shan's morning tears mourn the loss of hospitality, the sharing of the relaxing cabin in the mountains with so many others.

It's another day. I write the following report. It's mostly about emotions and spiritual perspective.

Leading up to our first trip back to the cabin, I held two small areas of hope, and allowed my imagination to see the happy return of our cars and some of my books, fly fishing and tying gear. These hopes - that the cars would work: on the drive down the canyon we'd discussed whether we could drive them out on that road, and the answer had been *Yes!* that only a little water would have entered the manhole: I'd given up a few books to water damage, but thought I'd handle that loss with grace because so much more would be okay - were dashed. The cars and, as far as we could tell, almost all of my tying materials and all of my books were soaked, ruined beyond salvage. A third area of hope, that Shan and Jessica would collect a few items they'd thought were dry because they were high, was fulfilled in part. (It turns out that hope of the unknown, like fear of same, is also irrational. Go figure.)

James 1:2 "My brethren, count it all joy when you fall into various trials, knowing that the testing of your faith produces patience."

I suppose the trials are various depending on the patience quota the tested one requires, and that accordingly glorify God. (I think all things bring God glory, and don't think what I can do or will do changes that a bit. He is God, and I am His, by the working of the strength of His might, not mine.) The individual is tested in order to trust God, in order to be free, and that others who have eyes to see and ears to hear may also choose to glorify God. The other option, as we've heard over and again, occurs when people hear about and focus on the trial, and then respond with, Oh! I'm so sorry.

Should we be sorry to build character? To build, or to learn, anything takes patience, which comes - character is produced concurrently with patience - when we individually or together, fall into various trials. Shan and

140

I, and Don and I, together and individually, experienced various trials. We were the source of a few for one another, too. Count it all joy!

James continues, "But let patience have its perfect work, that you may be perfect and complete, lacking nothing."

At least some of the various trials we fall into are not of our own making - I suppose we learn to avoid those of our own design and construction (tending to masochism, I struggle here) - which means all knowing God must know our plight and whether we'll respond by faith. Faith lets us know that the testing of our faith in fact will, and does, produce patience.

See?

It's easy to assign degrees of trial in order to compare and quantify; that's the wont of fallen, incomplete humans. Men compare injuries and scars; women other stuff. (When married, women compare their husband's behavior, who are always ready to assist the increase of patience in their wife: children of either gender do this for both mom and dad.) But a splash of cold water for a child, or one with childish character and patience, is as much a trial to them as a devastating flood is to another. Both occur on the road to becoming perfect and complete, to lacking nothing, if we listen.

Remember: it's not about the stuff, but about character, about patience.

Along the way, we often cry out, *How much more, oh God!?* as the Psalmists did. The cry is louder when we listen to noise instead of to God's Word, to His voice, to the One who inspired James to continue and to write, "If any of you lacks wisdom let him ask of God, who gives to all liberally and without reproach, and it will be given to him. But let him ask in faith, with no doubting, for he who doubts is like a wave of the sea driven and tossed by the wind."

I keep in mind - this must be in my mind because God puts it there, because He dwells in me by faith - that faith is God's gift, that He uses it to initiate, then to transact the relationship that allows me to know that I lack wisdom, then says, *Hey, just* ask for patience, while I count all the trials as joy. God initiates, and gifts faith that I may respond to Him, knowing all things work together for good.

During trials, various trials, God invades our being. Trials are where growth occurs, where, in the presence of God, I ask, *In light of what I now know, how shall I then live?* It's in trials that we see the need, know He is there, know He will fill us with Himself.

The will, my will, can choose to trust and obey - to count it all joy - and to gain patience so nothing is lacking, or no. But it takes patience to do so. And the decision to seek wisdom is going to be accompanied by trials of varying types, according to the need. God answers prayer. We have all that is required to walk, one step at a time, or to soar as we rise up on eagle's wings.

Oh well. Count it all joy. Or, be sorry, be normal, and complain.

Impatience seems like an easy enough choice, but as far as I can tell, patience lessons we need to travel Lack Nothing Avenue will be repeated until we say, by the act of our own will in response to God by faith, *Yes, Lord; yes.*

Proverbs 24:10 If you faint in the day of adversity, your strength is small.

After reading the verse from Proverbs, I read this in John 1:1-5: In the beginning was the Word, and the Word was with God, and the Word was God. He was in the beginning with God. All things were made through Him, and without Him nothing was made that was made. In Him was life, and the life was the light of men. And the light shines in the darkness, and the darkness did not comprehend it.

It's Monday morning, October 14, 2013, the day after our first return to the cabin. The morning weather oddly mirrors my own feelings. On opening the shades and looking east, I see dim light illuminating a clear sky punctuated by puffy clouds that portend a colorful sunrise. A few moments after the realization, Shan, ironing that day's work clothes, said, "It's raining or snowing."

I'd heard a sound that might indicate precipitation hitting glass, but thought it was kettle-heating-water-for-coffee-and-tea noises. That thought, combined with what I saw out the east window, made me ask, "What?"

"It's raining or snowing. I just heard something hit the window."

Looking east, I said, "It can't be raining; it's clear as a bell out there."

Shan said, "Oh? There are raindrops on the window," and when I turned to my left and looked out of the corner of my eye at the west-facing window, sure enough, I saw raindrops. I heard them, too. The sound wasn't coming from the kettle. Perspective is a curious thing, and what one is looking at often skews what they think, or assume, about what is going on in the adjacent vicinity.

Before we rose that morning, at about 5:45 a.m., Shan began to sob. It was a carryover from the night before. After arriving back at the farm after our Sunday foray to Drake, Shan, Jess, Blake and I had a group hug in what would become the kitchen, yet without its sink. We'd just unloaded the few surviving items we'd collected up there, and Jess and Blake were exhausted and ready to leave - he for Ft. Collins, and Jess to her Loveland apartment. In the hug, Shan cried, and said, "I know it's not about the stuff, but that little cabin was our home."Jess cried, too - a good thing for her: it had been her home, too.

After a span of silence moistened with tears, I said, "Home is where mom is," quoting the hot drink glass Jessica had given to Shan when we moved to the farm. We laughed.

Following this morning's rush of tears, and the proper span in silent embrace, I said, "What now?" Each tearful expression Shan experiences is followed by her attempt to reveal that which initiated it.

This is what she said. "That little cabin in the mountains was our home, and I was thinking about all of the people. The people who shared it with us, who visited, all of the cookouts and friends who got to spend some good, relaxing, quiet time on the mountain, accompanied by the sound of the river, the birds and the cool breeze in the trees."

And then she cried some more, verifying the depth of compassion that Shan feels and has for others.

The loss of the cabin was more about what others would miss than it was about us.

Even though such short, poignant, emotional responses are temporary surprises, they are honest responses to flashes of memory, or feelings of grief. But mourning, and correct grief pass like a few morning raindrops. A blue sky full of the sun's light brings new growth, and the promise it portends.

The view that met us after crossing the bridge

From the first, we realized that there is more than essential, obvious loss, and rarely have we felt like victims, like we were victimized by the flood. But those who victimize us as victims make another story.

In the months since I wrote that, I've come to realize that we're actually refugees; flood refugees. But that line of thought is not shared by media. It's probably too lame.

Later that day, after writing about the trip to Drake, I type and e-mail these notes. They take several separate transmissions because I attach many pictures to illuminate each page of text.

Hello,

I hope this comes out about right. It's the next in the ongoing reports I've been composing to try to keep you, our family and friends, abreast of what's going on. We started with the day the water started to rise, thinking that it would stop, continued after it didn't and we - Shan, Max, Bunny and I - were flown off the mountain and reunited with Jessica, then our short trials with finding a place to stay. Within a few days, we received an outpouring of affection from many of you, including many wishes and prayers, gifts of various sorts, and ongoing notes and emails to see what was up, to check in with us. I've also sent notes about the place it looks like we'll be staying for the foreseeable future, and a few others about this and that.

The other day, Shan and I returned to the farm to find the delightful, generous folks who own it trying to surprise us. They were installing a kitchen sink - you'll recall there was no kitchen - a fridge and a small cupboard that adds storage. Well, we ruined the surprise but got to enjoy their company! Delightful people with hearts full of love. I'm not surprised that they know and love Don, my brother. Other friends have lent us cars, given us stuff for the place, and tried in many ways to support our time of transition. Thanks to all of you, with all of our being. There is much more to write. I'm going to continue here, and try to explain a few things about yesterday - Sunday, October 13.

Last week, we heard that CDOT had completed a rough pioneer road from Estes Park to Drake. On Monday, a neighbor said it was rough, that only a 4-wheel drive vehicle would make it. I didn't think we should go down until we heard that this road was good enough to drive at least the Subaru, but preferably both cars, out. Word came later in the week, and we decided to head up on Sunday. Don agreed to drive his heavy duty truck - Don has been particularly generous and encouraging - and we'd decide whether or not the cars could drive back out.

Jess decided she wanted to come - the right thing for her since this was her home for quite some time - but that she really wanted Blake to come. Fair enough. One of Shan's coworker's friends decided to loan us a Suburban so we could haul stuff back. I announced that we'd leave at 7 a.m.

We left at 7:28 am - right on time, I guess, and drove to Boulder then up the canyon with that name to Nederland. Heading north on 72, we hit 7 near Allenspark, and continued along the Peak to Peak highway until we started down the mountain into Estes Park.

As you can see, there was visible water damage and lots of beauty along the way. The hired help was set - some were cute. After breakfast we headed down the canyon. The first set of pix were taken before.

We headed down the canyon. If you know the area, some of the pix will make an ordered sense, but chances are good that many of you won't know - and it doesn't matter.

As you'll see, the damage was apparent soon and often. Piles of once good stuff was piled along the road. For the most part, the upper portion of the canyon road was fine, in good shape. But then, we began to see road damage that morphed into complete road destruction.

Note the river and riparian habitat damage, too. [Picture p. 128] Of course the river will heal, once the people who will move it here and there, try to reform banks to keep it where they want it. Then, in the future, the river will once again go where it pleases, causing these folks to put monetary damage claims on what the river will do.

We began our trek with a sense of optimism for 2 things. (A few, we knew would be okay, and we planned to collect them.) The first were the cars. After the drive down, we'd determined that we could drive both out. We had it in our mind that we'd be back on the road in our own cars - you'll remember my truck was gone.

I've only put in one picture of the Subaru's carpet, but both cars were wet inside, and growing mold on the carpets and other parts. It was obvious that hope one was dashed, drowned in the high waters like so much else.

When we arrived at the cabin, after examining the cars, this is what we found. The pictures speak volumes, I think. There was more damage than we'd seen when we left, but I expected that due to the continuing rain and high water.

The second thing that I'd held out hope for had to do with the man hole and all of my tying stuff. There was a computer and external hard drive with all of the tying video I'd shot and hoped to produce and market; 34 years of hooks, materials and books; flies, pictures of trips and friends; some rare reels and favorite reels and fly rods; waders, boots, Jess' fishing gear; my dad's scouting stuff, and lots more.

We'd thought - and hoped - that maybe the water would only have come up a few inches, protected by the garage portion, all of the sand that settled there early on. That perhaps only a few books would be damaged, that much would be spared.

While Jess and Shan filled boxes with dishes, mementos and other items they wanted, Don and Blake tried to dig out the sand to open the door. No chance. So, Don broke the door open so we could see.

The pix say it all; nothing survived other than a few odds and ends that will have to be cleaned if they might be used at all. Books, feathers, flies, computer, cameras, etcc were all ruined.

When we finished loading the truck, everyone was tired, had sore backs and other body parts and frayed nerves. The drive out was different than the drive in.

When we got back to Don's, everyone washed the stinky mud from their hands and faces after changing clothes. All of the stuff it seems we'll be able to save was in the back of a Suburban.

One of two book shelves; this one was not upended, but inundated with water full of mud and sand

We ordered pizza, watched the end of the Broncos' game and then the news that followed to see what the game had been like.

During the newscast, they went live to a report from "near Drake" that was actually 8 miles above [west from] Drake, only a mile or so down [east] from Estes, where there was no damage to the road, good light and a great shot of massive destruction. The newscaster interviewed a couple from that area, continuing to show the devastation. When it showed the couple, under their names was the statement Flood Victims.

And it made me mad - more than angry. The victims are the people watching, I think - who like the idea of victimhood or something, I guess. Well, I don't want to pontificate on the irresponsible reporting that passes for journalism, and I'm not hot about it now - I've tried to learn to not let irrational crap mess with me like it once did.

It still seems that folks want us to feel like victims, though we don't, and won't, either. That many want me to feel sad for the loss of stuff, to mourn it - but I can't, and won't because it's only stuff. I don't have the piano, tying things and so on, but we could have all of that and Shan and I could have drowned - a perspective of little value, in fact. I guess I really don't care all that much about the stuff, and I can't manipulate up any anger or great distress at its loss. Sorry.

But this morning, Shan voiced - with full emotions! - what we both feel. We lost our home, but mostly it was the people who used this little mountain retreat to refresh, relax, fish, picnic, listen to the bubbling river and the cool breeze on a hot summer day; those who borrowed the cabin for a day or a week, who slept over, tied flies in the manhole, enjoyed a mental health day; who took pictures of hummingbirds on the feeder, saw deer or wild turkeys wander past; who found bighorn sheep on the mountainside, who were awed by the mystery of God's good creation and how it provided a salve to the hurry - cell phones didn't work there, and we had no TV reception (we still don't! GREAT!)

It's always been about people - our family, friends and strangers who stopped by because they needed a place to sleep for the night.

There's more to say, and I'm working at it, trying to make sense of all of the emotions, thoughts, responses and so on that have circled their boats on these floodwaters. I'm writing, making notes, trying to build a book with pictures, thoughts that Shan is writing, too, in order to encourage and build up those who will read.

I'd like your input via emails if you'd like to contribute. I'll answer when I can - I only make it to internet connections one time a day, and I might just slow down on that now. We'll see. So, please write and press on with your prayers to this end, that we would all know that all things are for God's glory and our freedom in Him - in Life.

Thanks for reading.

Love, Dale - I think Shan mostly approves.

PS: right now - please understand - I'm not very interested in talking about this. Thanks

While it was not my intent to stop people from writing - it was phone calls and the same questions over and again that I came to abhor - the end of my note sort of did keep people from responding. I suppose that was fair enough. By this time, too, it had been a month since we were flown off the mountain, and I had the feeling that a lot of early responders to my notes were worn out with writing, had lost interest in hearing any more old news. The media was reporting other disasters, deaths and destruction, interviewing new "victims" and so on. I suppose one can only take so much concentrated focus on one issue.

Y esterday, while we ate pizza at Don's before driving back to Loveland, we watched the TV news to hear reports about the Broncos' game, most of which we'd missed. Between hearing locker room heroes talk about their gridiron exploits, the newscasters announced a live flood report from near Drake.

"We now go live to Betty Sue, reporting from near Drake. So what's happening up there, Betty Sue?"

And Betty Sue (BS) answered, "I'm here near Drake where, as you can see...blah, blah, blah, blah, blah." The caption, Betty Sue near Drake, the scene, large iron girders, remnants of a destroyed bridge that spanned the Big T, and debris, including a car crammed under the destroyed bridge girders, hanging on it like so much garbage on a fence after a windstorm. Betty Sue expanded the damage with practiced journalistic jargon, and more blah, blah, blahing.

In reality, the spot was conveniently located about a mile down the canyon from Estes Park, at least 8 miles west from Drake, where the paved and undamaged road offered easy access for BS, the camera operator and driver, with a lovely shot to keep the horror of the flood's destruction right in front of the audience, who apparently had to be put back into their spots after the euphoria of the Broncos' victory. How many were also eating pizza? Waiting for more locker room banter? For the promised weather report? They mustn't be permitted such ease!

To enhance the story, the horror of it all, Betty Sue had interviewed a couple who might have lived in the canyon. Under their names, the caption Flood Victims was flashed on the screen, and reappeared each time the short clips of their faces appeared on screen.

I knew I felt sad after our trip back, but I was irritated by this report, perhaps in part because I don't watch TV news - I don't watch TV, other than for an occasional game. My irritation was primarily due to the reason I stopped watching TV: irresponsible, demeaning reports like this. (That, and stupid commercials.)

Looking east now - it's a little after 8 a.m.; Shan's at work - I see sunshine on treetops, but also dark clouds like low hanging fruit; now, there are a few raindrops on the east-facing window. To the west, patches of blue peek through higher clouds that are white and light - the sky switched places! If the clouds lift, they'll reveal high peaks on the Continental Divide that hold new snow. Jess and Blake are drooling for their first ski/snowboard outing of the year. (One area, A Basin, opened yesterday, four days earlier than last year!)

On Sunday, Don emoted that he was sad. The flood and its aftermath was physically and emotionally exhausting, and we were both tired. Don wears his emotions on the outside more than I do; fatigue exacerbates them for each of us. Internally, I ruminate, think and argue positions, take both sides when I can, and try to figure out what the right thing is. Often, though, I take and defend my own position more than I ought.

I interpreted Don's sadness as anger towards me - an unfair, but common response on my part. It started before the drive down the canyon, increased along the way and heightened dramatically when we looked at the ruined cars, cabin and its contents. The condition of other homes, the road and the river itself didn't lighten our load. It was Don's first look, my first time back after I watched the flood progress and then destroy our neighborhood. This was my first view of the rest of it.

I had a little hope but very little enthusiasm about going to the cabin. I started ruminating with anticipation of this day when, a week earlier, I heard that crews had completed a rough pioneer road over the areas where Highway 34 had been damaged or washed out. It was inevitable that we'd have to go back and face the consequences of the flood, but I wasn't at all happy about actually going back. My rumination led to a mild malaise. For the most part, I thought going back was a big fat waste of time. With the condition of my back, hand and other physical issues, there was very little I could do, and like I said, I also had little hope about recovering any stuff. But I knew that being with Shan and the others, offering support and helping make decisions, had value, that I must go.

While I looked at the malaise objectively, I still felt blue. As usual, my common sense and the malaise battled one another. I wanted someone to talk with me, to help me work it through on the outside, but knew that would not - in fact could not - happen. There's no one I can share my emotions with. This was confirmed on Tuesday of the week before the trip to review and collect stuff, when Don and I met for lunch in Loveland. He drove down to the Valley - a 2-plus hour drive each way instead of the usual one of about 40 minutes - to pick up an order of stone and other supplies for a job he was doing.

I told him I was in a malaise, but he didn't know what that meant. And at the time, Don was exuding an *I'm really happy* mien, and I knew there was no messing with that.

I tried to talk with Shan, too, but she was empty after her long workdays, troubled with coming to grips with things, very distant with me, at times judgmental and bossy, and interrupted me when I tried to answer a question or make a comment on the lingering *What now?* questions we had. It was fair enough, too. We're in love; these things happen. But like I said, I would not, could not, talk it out with Shan or Don.

But my inability to express the malaise, no doubt partly due to the inability of Shan and Don to listen to it - there were no other reasonable possibilities, sad to say - caused the gentle bubbling to begin boiling. The malaise increased and darkened; I slept less and became more fatigued.

Curious opportunities to help others by doing specific things - I helped a young author list his books on Amazon, discussed specific ideas with people in the coffee shop, met and talked about being a dad with a young father - energized and wore me out. Focusing on others always dispels thoughts for myself. Funny how that works, eh?

Before we left the cabin to go back to Don's on Sunday, the malaise turned to sadness, and then came the blowup with Don.

After Sunday pizza, but before we left, Don and I had a long hug. The hug was loving medicine that provided an unspoken but therapeutic salve to both of our open wounds. Neither of us spoke a word. I kissed his forehead. We patted one another on the back. The hug spoke volumes above the mutual yelling match we'd shared earlier by the cabin; both of us needed the yelling release and the loving hug.

Don and I talked again after our trip back. One of his comments, made in awe and wonder but from a practical perspective, had to do with the lack of dirt and soil that was left around our - and many other - properties in the wake of the flood.

When Don first saw the pictures of the cabin, he said, "Based on what I know about that structure and what I see, the only way to proceed is to scrape it and start over." We talked about cost. He wondered about the pump, vault and leach field. I said I thought the well and pump should be okay because the water didn't get there - a statement that later proved to be incorrect - but wasn't sure of the vault; I couldn't imagine the grey water leach field was still there with no dirt left and all. (On Sunday, I pointed at and said, "The river flowed through where the leach field used to be.")

We wondered where fresh dirt to rebuild the landscape would be found, and talked about who would take responsibility for hauling it in when it became available. (Even gravel and sand fill are at a premium. Estes Park is mining Lake Estes, and Loveland is tearing out Idylwilde Dam to get gravel and sand that was in that small reservoir.) No answers, only questions, conversations, speculation. When Don first mentioned the scrape, I tried to imagine getting a machine to the cabin. During our visit, it was clear that very large, powerful machines had been moving rocks and debris because the river had been moved and was flowing under the bridge in an ugly, but practical ditch. A small lake by the cabin held water. Where the tracked equipment had lumbered, dug and pushed, sand and gravel filled spaces between stones and rocks. Boulders, depending on their weight and mass, had been pushed or shoveled into piles, or left where the water deposited them.

We saw Chris during our trip to Drake on October 13. She was wandering around the neighborhood with a friend, while her boyfriend drove a replacement vehicle they'd bought. She said, "I'm doing better every day!" It was good to see her, good to hear her say so!

On Friday and Saturday after our first trip back to the cabin, Shan and I clean and repair stuff we salvaged. We wear gloves and masks - and maintain a sense of humor and perspective - use harsh cleansers and sanitizer, and lots of water while exerting physical and emotional energy. It's awful. Trying to clean things that will be forever scarred arouses new emotions. Shan is a hard worker, and focuses on the task at hand, works diligently to clean everything as thoroughly as she can. She keeps me at it, too, even though I have very little enthusiasm for this task.

In reality, a few of the now clean but still scarred items are useful, and I'm glad to have them! On Monday, Shan returns to work, to the stability of her regular schedule while I continue to write, make and answer calls. I'm disappointed by the lack of trust I've witnessed from the government and other bureaucratic entities with whom we've had to deal. Of course I realize there is enmity between government and the governed: they despise one another. (Larimer County earned my lack of trust during previous events; the votes are still out on how they'll handle the flood's aftermath, but it's not looking good.)

ROADWORK

Highway 34 was partially damaged or destroyed. Over some stretches, the river, after destroying it, made what was a roadbed into a riverbed so its water could flow there. In other stretches, after rising and ruining asphalt and the roadbed, the river receded into its original course and left sand, rock and gravel swaths where the road had been. Other stretches of roadway were undermined, collapsed, got washed away or stayed as they were. We've heard similar reports concerning Highways 36, 7, 72 and 119, many County roads, including CR 43 from Drake to Glen Haven, the street that follows the North Fork. Jamestown, and the road there, are in terrible condition.

Much attention is being paid to the roads and bridges that were in the flood's way, part of what they now call its aftermath. (What sort of math is that?) After all, residents, visitors, vacationers and commerce flow on these roads and cross the bridges that span the rivers, while crews who maintain and repair each make their living working on the roads and bridges. They, and imported workers, have plenty of work for the foreseeable future. As damages were assessed, pictures and videos collected and dispensed, the experts and accountants fired up their calculators, made calculations, and stated how many millions of dollars and how much time it would take to repair and rebuild roads and bridges. Many suggested it would take years! The Governor of Colorado said 34 and 36 would be complete by December 1, 2013. People laughed; pontificators scowled; most doubted.

After the announcement, the appointed manager said the road might be gravel, rough, or, in certain areas one lane, but the canyon would be open to through traffic by December 1. In fact, that manager and those he hired, including the contractors, produced a remarkable feat. State Highway 34 was finished - rebuilt, paved and with painted lines - and open to two-way traffic before Thanksgiving! The work is seamless, the road as good or better than what was destroyed. Laughing people, scornful pontificators and doubters changed their tune; many now drive the road. Once again, people take the thoroughfare for granted, which is a good thing. A few weeks after it was open to vehicle traffic, 34 was reopened to bicyclists. Amazing.

For perspective, a report noted that one particular construction worker, who volunteered for the job - the report said he was from Tennessee! - worked forty-eight straight fourteen-hour days. This was not unusual. The organization, management, and focused execution of the job by committed, hard-working people resulted in what many now describe as a miracle. The weather was perfect, too. It didn't rain. I wonder if this kind of focus, determination and hard work will be put forth to assist displaced residents? So far, there is a lot of talk and very little action: the answer is *no*.

I also wonder about the trout streams, the riparian habitat and life that they support. Trout streams and their environs teem with life, in spite of the damage done by pollution made by nearby inhabitants, roads and the commerce they ply. Nature thrives.

SECOND TRIP

On a Tuesday nearly two months after the flood, five weeks after we first had access to the cabin, I finally meet the FEMA inspector at the cabin. Jess rides up with me, a comfort on just our second uncomfortable trip back to what had been our home. Again, I dislike being there, dislike the drive down the canyon from Estes; both bring gloom into my heart. The drive out is no treat, either.

In the past, I've occasionally suffered what I call an impending sense of doom, and the gloominess now feels similar, but is not the same. Perhaps this is due to the intimate knowledge of gloom's source: the damage the floodwater caused to my beloved trout stream and so many homes, including our own, and so much more. It's the doom's reality, no longer impending but now finished; its remains are gloom incarnate.

Jess and I meet the young FEMA inspector as he walks to the cabin. He wants to see my driver's license and a copy of our homeowners' insurance policy so he knows this is actually our place, that we're the people who called FEMA multiple times over a period of two months to schedule this appointment, during which each time I had to give all of my vital statistics before the person on the phone would talk to me about anything other than me identifying who I was. Why, I wonder, would any one fake such a thing? How could anyone other than me and the inspector know of this meeting? What is it that makes bureaucrats design a system that is so thoroughly demeaning, especially during already unsettling circumstances? I have no answers, other than for the creation and sustenance of an entity, and to exercise manipulative control in order to express power. After presenting the required items to enter my own home, we show him in. On the way, I say, "There are a few particulars that I'd like to..........," but before I complete the sentence, he cuts me off, saying, "All we cover is basic living necessities: a roof, bed, heat and so on."

"I was under the impression that FEMA grants kicked in to cover what insurance and SBA loans don't," I said. (We knew immediately that both denied us.)

He said, "Our max grant is about thirty-thousand dollars," and I slump, not so much disappointed, but wondering, once again, about God's appointment. (It's from Phil Keagy's song; he sings *change one letter, then you'll see. His appointment...*) It's easy enough to be disappointed by the world's attacks, its antics - there seem to be an abundance of them just now - but I have hope in what God will appoint. Once again, He keeps me from collapse.

A quick look inside finds a few kitchen cabinet doors ripped off their jambs, and the cabinets' contents strewn across the kitchen floor, on top of the mud. For good measure, and to identify his work, the bear also left two piles of scat on top of the mud on the living room floor, once again skewing the common perception that wild bears only shit in the woods. The answer to the question of where bears shit, then, is, like many things: it depends. *We'll get back to you, but first, could you identify yourself for your security?* Of course bears live by instinct and shit when they need to, wherever they want; bureaucracies function by insidious design.

That scene, combined with the initial interaction with the FEMA inspector, is enough for me. I walk back out to the borrowed Yukon we drove, open the door, climb in and sit down. Jess continues to wander a bit, I suppose wondering if this will be her final trip up to the cabin, her home for the past six years. Within short order, the young inspector is at the car's window with a list of questions: did you have this, that, and so on. After entering the info into the computer he carries, he says, "This looks like a max grant to me. You should hear back in a few days." He says this with what sounds like aloof glee to my ears, as though the announcement will solve all of our problems.

Then, with sincerity, he wishes us good luck - I don't believe in luck, but you probably already know that - and Jessica and I leave. Thirty minutes; that's how long it was from engine off to engine on. I spent that long and longer on many of the numerous phone calls to schedule this meeting.

I suppose the shortness of our stay, at least in part, was founded on knowing that Don was assembling a group of friends who volunteered to help us on the ensuing Friday, and I knew I'd be back in three days. (I didn't consider this time up as a return trip as much as a requirement for aid.) But there was the gloom, too, which played its role well.

On our return to Estes, Jessica and I meet Don at Sweet Basilica for lunch. We take our time, then follow Don to a repair place, where he leaves his truck to have the windshield replaced, before driving him back home and then visiting with Larraine. We discuss the Friday trip to the cabin, set a few guidelines. On our way back to the farm, and before we arrive, I receive a phone call from the one helpful, sincere FEMA representative I've met. James tells me that we've been granted the full amount that FEMA offers, but we won't hear about it for a few days. He just wants to let me know the decision is already made. He knew that I became a skeptic after calling the FEMA help line, which was nothing of the sort, multiple times to schedule the inspection; that my skepticism remained after finding him, because he had to call three more times to get the inspection scheduled and confirmed. And now, within a few hours after an eight-week wait, the thing is finished. James, my FEMA friend, says, "That's all we can do," before listing other things that we should expect. FEMA will put other nonprofit, private and public entities in touch with us; they will offer help. (None of that has happened.)

The details of Friday's festivities came together over the next two days. Don plans to haul his Bobcat and its attachments down to the cabin, where he'll use the machine to dig out the sand and debris that filled the carport and blocked the garage. The three men and one woman, he says, and Larraine - Don's wife - will be ready to leave Estes at 9 a.m. Friday, and will be ready to work. Shan makes arrangements to once again borrow the Suburban, but the best news comes when Brittany decides to fly out from Kansas City to see us and to help! Shan would, at last, be able to hug our middle girl, completing the trifecta of daughter hugs. Yeah!

A tying friend of mine also joined us, and after a variety of delays on Friday morning, we made it to Estes, then to the cabin, and finally started to work. On the drive down, it was obvious that the roadwork had been ferocious, steady and well-managed. I wondered who sat in the director's chair and kept all of the moving pieces of equipment, people and entities moving at the right time to the right place. What a great job they were doing! As a matter of fact, sections of the road between Estes and Drake that had been rough, rugged single lanes on the first trip were paved; center lines were being painted. The road was seamless and perfect!

One of Don's friends brought a generator and we tried to get the well's pump to work so we could rinse stuff we gathered from the house. Leaving the mud and the odor up there was a good idea. But this experiment failed; the pump didn't work. Instead, we used 26 gallons of water that

Brittany and I had bought the day before, after I picked her up at DIA. But the electricity we generated ran lights that helped us see stuff in the garage and in the manhole, and that was great. The light, as always, dispelled darkness and cut through the gloom. Even though it revealed the facts of damage, illustrated the destruction of our stuff, like Jesus' Light does sin, I love the Light.

While Shan, the other women, and a few men worked to salvage items in the cabin, Don ran the Bobcat, moved dirt, buried a six-inch steel pipe that would move water under our works - the small road he made from the dirt and sediment in the carport - and created a clear, flat work area under the carport.

My friend extricated garden hand tools - shovels, rakes, an axe, spud bar, crowbars and so on - and we used them to move items, to shovel mud and sand into the Bobcat's bucket. Several of us chopped up, broke apart and moved away other once-dear items out of the Bobcat's path. It took a long time to get to the garage door, but once there, it was broken apart and Don bucketed out yards of mud, sand and debris from inside.

Shan climbs out of the hole that was our yard while other generous volunteers help salvage a few items we'll clean later

Much of the debris was material we meant to recycle that was dislodged before the floodwater blended it into the mud and sand. But we sifted out a fly reel - there should have been two, but we never found the second - two more crow bars, other hand tools and a few other useful odds and ends. We carried out large tubs of tying materials, Jess' new skis, two snowboards,

and other items we thought we might be able to clean and use again, into the area Don had cleared in the carport. We set up a makeshift table on which to clean stuff, and made further decisions on what should be cleaned, what should be discarded. Whether or not any of it actually survives and returns to usefulness remains unclear.

And then, we finally got to the manhole; it held my treasure trove of books and fly fishing goodies. Two of the men walked in and started shoveling out mud. I knew there were several small items that I wanted to find, so I asked them to wait by the door while I waded and looked through the muck. And I did find several rare reels, boxes of feathers we could clean - others, we just left - Jess' fishing vest and fly reel, and other items. I hoped to find the second Renzetti tying vise, and we did. It was on the seat of a chair that held up one of the two very heavy, upended, but still full bookshelves. When we lifted the shelf, I was surprised that the vise had been supporting all of the case's weight. It showed water damage, but the vise still turned and looked like it would work. (It does.) We also collected other odds and ends. I tried to find classic salmon hooks - many were antiques - but didn't have much luck because they were apparently buried in the mud. In the process, I examined and tossed a variety of other stuff.

One of the men climbed around on the bookshelf. I asked, "Do you see the computer box or an external hard drive back there?"

He didn't. But after looking, lifting, sifting and so on, he finally found both, caked in mud and still moist. My friend, and adopted son, Keith says he knows people who can recover the data stored on the drives, which has thousands of photos and hours of tying and fishing video I shot. I hope that works. We'll see. (It didn't!) The video cameras were destroyed - water poured out of them - and, as I'd expected, all of my books, collected, lent and read over the past five decades, were ruined. I looked at the spines of many, thought of authors I'd met, the information I'd gleaned and the enjoyment I'd had when I read and shared with others; I sighed.

On Saturday, the next day, Shan, Brittany and two of Brittany's friends were outside in the farm driveway where they washed, cleaned, sanitized and coddled some of the stuff we salvaged. They worked hard; their fingers got very cold. (Shan recalls the scent of the brown mucky goo and the continued gloom. I spent that day feeling blue at a book signing I'd agreed to before the flood. Blue in the aftermath of the trip back to the cabin, the thought of the girls cleaning stuff, and the fiasco the signing turned out to be. Oh well.) I question how much of the stuff will actually be useful, and still find myself with mixed feelings about the things we lost, as well as the things we saved. I am a little sad at the loss - mostly, I suppose, similar to how I feel about the loss of the cabin: what it and lost stuff had done and still could do for others - but I'm still pretty much unable to muster any deep sense of mourning because it's all just stuff.

I also wonder about all of the time we've spent trying to recover items, and then clean them, especially, for me at least, because all of that time has been taken away from writing this book. Still, the votes are out, and we'll have to wait and see how it - the book, the stuff, where we'll live, what happens next - all works out. We know it will, know that which matters will be clear, that we'll know what to do when it does matter.

Sadly, the mass of phone calls from government and insurance entities continued to come to both of our phones. I've answered and spoken with the callers, who often also left messages with or actually talked with Shan. When they left a message, in the moment, Shan has called back, and two different conversations with either the same or different representatives confused issues for everyone. Shan doesn't need this confusion, and I try to protect her, ask her to tell callers to speak with me. And the stress, the disappointment based on the rudeness, unhelpfulness, incompetence or downright stupidity I am forced to listen to, is difficult to deflect. It tries my sensitivity and patience, and I wonder if that trial will result in more patience. (It always does.) I guess we'll see.

I maintain a perspective that says time heals or eventually solves every issue, while I know that each entity will do what their computers' scripts tell them to say and to do, that it will be very hard to get to a person who knows anything and will help. For the most part, the rest favor their entity rather than their client or customer: all of the numbers attached to conversations verify this: case number, disaster area number, and so many other numbers. Still, dealing with bureaucracies and the people who work in them remains a challenge. *Exercise patience. Endure. Persevere.*

That's what we did - continue doing - through the conclusion of our second trip to the cabin. It was tough seeing our stuff so ruined, but tougher washing and trying to repair that which we rescued. The stench permeated everything. It made me sick.

Still, the sun rose, Max anticipated and ate his meals with relish, Shan worked and I wrote and started tying a few flies. Hosting weekly wet fly tying sessions has been fun. Even though we're aware of an ongoing sense of being unsettled, we know thanksgiving at having a place to stay.

We know the recovery process will last for a very long time or several years, whichever comes first; I don't think it's affecting our love and compassion for one another, for our family, and for others. As is the case with any profound loss, images of what was, what is gone, flash into our minds and mess with our emotions. We respond, then press on, doing what we can do each day.

PERSPECTIVE

Shan: "We don't base our well-being on stuff, but I'm mourning things that were part of my life." Then she specifically mentioned the coat tree. A simple, old, pretty thing that was meaningful because of how long it was, and where it went, with her.

W̲ithin short order, our unwanted celebrity, which surged during the flood and after we got off the mountain, waned. Even though it hadn't dawned on me before this event, we, like the other darlings of disaster, became victim celebrities. The oddity increased as I thought about people we knew who embraced a gee-I'm-in-awe-and-need-to-call/write/email-so-I-can-participate-in-your-grief   mien. Media train us to it, and of course we learn, embrace and participate in it until we forget, or fresh blood takes priority. I came to ignore previously unknown people who wanted to join this crowd when they found out I was, in their minds, a flood victim. Sorry.

For the record, we neither felt like celebrities nor victims during or after the flood. We still don't. Yes, it damaged and destroyed; yes, it caused chaos and disrupted habits and styles. But being in the flood - or another similar event: Colorado also has wild fires; Louisiana, hurricanes; and so on - was an experience that comes to a few people all over the world, every day of the year, while elsewhere, the steady beat of normalcy goes on. And one visited us. (As I write this, my friend and our benefactor, Bud, has battened down his bayou hatches and taken family and friends into the bosom of his heart and home while a powerful tropical storm pounds south Louisiana. In an e-mail yesterday, Bud assured me that he's been through this many times, that it will be nothing like Katrina, the minx whose shadow won't go away.)

Since, I've also learned that other than by experiencing a surprising disaster yourself it's not possible to relate to another from afar. We try - I know I did when others told me of an experience, or when I read about this tornado or that surprise ice storm. I imagined what it would be like. But the fact of the matter is that I couldn't really imagine what it was like. In part, this was because I only saw snippets of the events, heard short versions of what occurred, or saw what media decided I should see. I didn't live in it, go through it, hear the sounds, sniff the scents, see the torrents, feel the quivering of the earth or taste the acrid flavor of the present doom of normalcy.

And then there is that which is ongoing. What those out-of-the-know but in-the-loop refer to as recovery. At what I started to refer to as the refugee center - FEMA's Disaster Relief Center - right off the bat young volunteers asked, "So how is your recovery coming along?" Even though it was a fair and perhaps thoughtful question, I found that I had no answer. What did the question mean? How can you quantify the loss or ruin of ninety-nine percent of your stuff, especially when there is little to no chance that it will be replaced? (Another thing I tried to visualize, but now know I couldn't, after seeing a charred chimney where a home full of life was recently being lived.) We feel vulnerable and unsettled, as any refugee must.

I'll admit that, in times past, I thought I'd be fine if someone stole my fly vest and all of the flies I'd tied that filled - let's see, one, two, three, four-five-six--nine boxes at the least were in the vest that drifted away in the truck; all were stuffed with flies. Most were dry flies, because that's what I fish. In my after-the-boxes-were-gone imagination, I wondered what I would tie, carry and use. Now and then, I'd have a discussion with an angling friend about how we'd replace, organize and repopulate our fly boxes; and so on. A fresh start sounded good. In fact, I'd started fresh in fits and starts throughout the previous 34 years of tying and fishing, buying new boxes and filling them with this and that, or tying specific patterns for specific trips. I almost always tied a few fresh flies before and or after a trip, even one that took me out the front door for an hour or two of fishing on the T. *Yeah*, I thought, *starting over would be fine*.

But that was when I could still tie a dozen or so flies an hour, back when both hands still worked and fly tying was a joy for me. Tying nearly one-handed is tough - tying is still fun, mind you - and the thought of replacing thousands of flies has become daunting. I'd even become more cautious about giving flies away, which made me sad: I love sharing. Regardless, now, all of my boxes and the flies the boxes carried are gone.

By the time Shan and I got off the mountain, and when I could connect to the internet, I found that tying friends from around the world who were aware of our dilemma were already collecting and sending hooks and tying materials to Chuck, who offered to serve as broker. They all knew how close Chuck and I are, that we fish together often, and talk a lot about tying flies. To say that I felt flabbergasted would be an understatement. I'd already thought about writing this book, but shortly after the outpouring of affection by my tying friends, as well as so many others, I decided the book would be one of thanks to everyone who supported Shan and I after the flood. (The book won't be enough.)

Now and then, this is soon after the flood, soon in the process of figuring out what in the world is going on with what seems like so many things, I've had a short surge of enthusiasm to tie a few flies, to fill new fly boxes; I even bought a new fly box, a few hooks and some materials. But the key word is short, for my enthusiasm quickly waned. After receiving the first gift of tying goodies from Chuck - Keith brought them to the farm - two weeks after we were evacuated, and after Shan found and for fifty bucks bought a dandy old roll top fly tying desk, I sat down, assembled the tools, adjusted the new tying vise, and tied one dry fly. That was all I had, all I could do. That was it. The next day, Chuck and I met in Longmont. He had a pile of donated classic salmon tying materials, and had selected and organized a few for me, wanted me to have them so I could work out some of my emotions while tying one of these complex, time consuming flies. Fly tying has always been a delight, often serving as a balm for thoughtful introspection. But I didn't even look at the materials for weeks after our meeting. Maybe I'll be able to tie when the book is finished.

WRITING

As it turns out, and apart from popular materialism and the quantifying nature it receives, most of this is not about stuff. I mean I do have a sense of loss, but little sadness for the things that are gone. Still, I'm starting to think the malaise that I now feel is a form of emotional shock for me. I'm not depressed - and I know how that feels! - it's just that all I'm really aware of, or motivated to do, is write the story. I continued to answer emails and phone calls, to jump through bureaucratic hoops, and comfort others, but it's the story that's haunted me. Edits are emotionally tough.

My answer to "So what are you going to do now?" is, *I'll write.*

The ongoing malaise feels both emotional and physical, but not spiritual or intellectual. I'm still thinking fast and in straight lines, but bumble words now and then, as I have done for some time. I think it's fatigue, which the malaise probably feeds; they probably feed each other. While there are specific, bright times when I'm pretty sure I know God's presence - someone once said if you thought you felt God moving within, you should be sure what you felt wasn't the pizza you ate the night before - but regardless of my feelings, I have confident knowledge and belief, based on His gift of faith that allows belief, that I do discern the difference between indigestion and God's Spirit moving within. That, and believing that Truth and time go hand in hand, keeps me stable, keeps me going. I haven't had much emotional support, and the physical pain I have continues to do its demeaning work on my system. But writing about the event, and the exploratory writing about God's love and grace, is definitely useful, brings definitive perspective. Thinking about others does, too. It's a type of worship.

Even though it can be painful, I love the Light, and am aware of my mind being renewed. Both seeking Light and the renewal of the mind involve volition, the purposeful decision to do, and to have each done. In Romans, Paul, after beseeching his readers, by the mercies of God, to present their bodies a living sacrifice, holy and acceptable to God, which is your reasonable service, says, "And do not be conformed to this world, but be transformed by the renewing of your mind, that you may prove what is that good and acceptable and perfect will of God."

If, as I've been told, the intellect - the mind - checks and controls emotions, then the directive Paul gives - *do not be conformed but be transformed by the renewing of your mind* - bears pondering and must become more insistent during irrational emotional activity. Emotional malaise happens, but allowing it to control, like a drug, rather than being filled with and obedient to the Spirit of God that dwells within each Christian, within me, is a bad choice that offers one's body as a corpse to the world, rather than as a living, holy, acceptable sacrifice to God.

I hadn't thought of it quite like that before writing the words just then. Interesting. There's another *How shall I then live* arrow for the quiver.

Writing, for me, is restful; is exhausting. They go hand in hand. It's also mentally and spiritually invigorating.

During college summers, I loved framing a house because the manifestation of the work appeared fast and became evident as floors, walls, a roof and so on took shape, like a skeleton against the sky. The work was quick and purposeful, as we did one thing over and over until the sum of each action formed a lasting structure. During breaks, and lunch, and at day's end, I was tired, sore and happy. Often, I thought about the home that would be created within the structure I was building. The rote-like flow of measuring and laying out lumber, pounding nails, applying a brace to hold things together, and so on, was restful and exhausting, but there was something tangible to see. I knew we'd accomplished something good, something meaningful. And the weekly pay, which I always deposited in my college savings account - the only account I had - was a thrill.

I write with an ink pen on lined sheets of paper, one word at a time, grouping them into sentences that I put on every other line. That way, when I cross out errors, rather than hitting the backspace button and retyping as on a computer, I just write the changes in the blank spaces. Writing like this slows me down, but also allows me to think about, then see each word take shape, one pen stroke at a time. (Typing in a word processing program causes too many stutters because my perfectionist bent makes me edit too often.) It's like laying out studs by the plate that's marked with a line and an X to show where each stud should be nailed, one nail at a time while building a wall. As a laborer, I nailed the wood where the boss marked it; and I write the words as they come, as it were, inspired by God. Delightful, invigorating, exhausting, all in one.

What shall I then write?

The next thing, one word at a time.

Thoughts and emotions rattle and flow through my mind, and I trust that I have the vocabulary and skill to record them, that with edits and further considerations, they will be clear and communicate, that they'll fill a need while entertaining and encouraging those who read.

The process is like what's been going on for the past forty years or so as God, by His grace, inspires, and as I respond by faith to His call to renew my mind. Often muddled thoughts are either discarded or given order, one at a time, while my emotions bubble as in a caldron that I don't want to explode. On Christ the solid rock I stand; upon that foundation He builds and makes me complete.

In addition to the ongoing fatigue I suffer due to the enduring pain I have, and the lack of sleep I've had for the past couple of months, there is a lot of stuff to process as a result of the flood. (We're still unsettled on May Day 2014 as I edit.)

John records of Jesus in John 1:2-3 that "He was in the beginning with God. All things were made through Him, and without Him nothing was made that was made." Elsewhere, Spirit inspired and directed a faithful man to write that *In Him all things were made, move and have their being.* My interpretation of from Him, and through Him and to Him are all things is that Jesus is the Source, Sustainer and Future of everything. He gives: indeed HE IS LIFE!

This - the flood, and so on - is all in the purview of His will. And I have a choice - my own free will - to say and believe *Thy will be done*, to act on and out of that, or to be conformed to the world that shirks and avoids the Light that illuminates all things. The world encourages and instills victimhood, thrives in suffering while bitching about it, and builds institutions to create, solve, and then recreate new problems.

How shall I live?

Well, not out of the malaise, even though the malaise is still lurking, ever ready to cloud my mien, and rain on my head. The devil may want me to luxuriate in my grief, to curse God for my victimhood, loss, inconvenience and so on, but I will not do that. I could - it's right there, a tangible temptation - but I will not, by God's grace.

How often, *I can't do* such and such is, in fact, *I won't do*. Observing and knowing the difference matters. The act of one's will is different than an *I can't* cop out. And how often I've heard, *I'm just doing my job*, along the way.

W hat is normal, anyway? How does normal sound, feel, look, smell and taste? What makes so many people wish me a return to normalcy?

Things will get back to normal! they write. Or, *I hope things get back to normal!* And, *I pray that normalcy will return!* All are said emphatically, in what often feels like a demanding tone. *I insist you return to normal!* Of course, this is how I take it, which doesn't mean that's how it's intended.

These wishes and hopes, whether sent with good intentions or not, feel like another type of imposition. What's wrong with experiencing a season of suffering, want or need? And I wonder if God invades lives during what, to them, feels like normalcy. Frankly, I'm well aware of being abnormal in most ways, so my comments on normal probably aren't.

Does normal fit into comfort zones of one's own making? Is rote such a zone? Acting out of what we expect of ourselves, or out of preconceived expectations we imagine or know or assume or have been imposed on us by others?

Much of what's come to be called *living the Christian life* seems like rote, and varies from one denomination to another, by geographic area, age, style, and so on, as groups and individuals create lists that define what living the Christian - or liberal, or conservative - life means to them.

Maybe normal is what we strive for to make a place that fits us. Normal smells like this, is accompanied by this music or that set of sounds - which now includes ear-buds or ear-plugs - looks like this, tastes like someone's cake and feels good to me. *Hey, I gotta' be me!* (The cell phone texting/gaming madness feeds the obsession of selfish indulgence.)

It seems like many try to manipulate circumstances in order to manipulate themselves away from discomfort, irregularity and the unexpected. The manipulation takes on several forms that include human made religiosity, control, games, addictions and grabbing the gusto; or whatever. All are fed by fear, beer and car commercials, tawdry opinions written by people with whom we agree, political parties and their position papers, and now also look-the-same-while-traveling popular thoroughfares because chain restaurants and stores - always the same, know what to expect: it's comfortably normal, after all - are all that's left.

Normal people - rich and poor, educated and uneducated, social or antisocial, religious or not, and so on - all seem to complain about their lot, anyway. Maybe complaining is part of normalcy. Put on the spot about their complaint, people tend to defend their style, and justify staying in the same place. "Well," they might say, "it's a regular check and pays the bills," while continuing to whine about the job, boss, spouse, government, etcetera.

"But you were just complaining about your boss," one might mention. "Why don't you find a new job?"

Possible retorts include, *My wife/husband would kill me*; *What if I didn't - or I'm afraid I couldn't - find another job or the right thing?* Or, *I just like to complain,* or, change the subject with *Hey, how about those Broncos?* Maybe it's a change of subject people want, which is easier than talking about the depths of their own, or another's, despair. Maybe the *I hope things get back to normal,* is their way of saying, *That flood is old news. I want to move on now, to be normal again.*

I've often thought that one of the key statements of the 1960s - the one that goes, *I think people can do whatever they want as long as they don't hurt someone else,* meant, still means, *I want to do whatever I want to do whenever I want to do it, and I don't care if it hurts anyone else or not; just leave me alone.* In the 1960s, many shook their heads with disdain over this statement. Today, it's an assumed, manifest position.

While that might be normal for some, it's not for me. Still, even though most people keep trying, it is a blessing when they escape normalcy and enter into Life.

Being abnormal puts me - and maybe you, too, in your own delightful ever-morphing style - in an odd position. Through the years, I've realized that following popular, pat-sounding statements to what seem to be their logical end results in emptiness, meaningless fodder, falsehood or bold faced lies. As a result, I tend to discard and not use them for myself, or confront them when others spout them. Most, in the guise of being profound, and usually spoken with the proper tone required to be, or to feel, profound, are phony. Phony profundity.

It is what it is has become popular, and functions to end a conversation. But if it were true, or even accurate, the thing that is doesn't need the statement to be what it is. In fact, the statement does nothing to inform or clarify, but is a lazy cop-out, a catchall to avoid meaningful discussion about a specific issue.

The statement that got me shushed when I started to confront the shorter Sheriff's Advocate, was her continued banter to Shan and me, that *We all fear the unknown.*

As soon as I started to respond, Shan, who has heard my argument over and again, knew what was coming, and shushed me - an unfortunately-for-me normal thing - and I obediently shushed. (I shut my eyelids before rolling my eyes.) The advocate, encouraged by Shan's shushing, repeated it and started plodding through her lists of the unknown, again piling on how frightened we victims should feel - being afraid must be part of victimhood - so she could feel good about herself for telling us how we should feel and trying to fix it so we felt - normal, was it?

How can anything that is unknown possibly be listed if it is unknown? How can the list be enumerated? (We know all about the flood, but we were never afraid of it.) I just don't think it's possible to fear that which we don't know. Maybe what we fear is fear itself, that which President Roosevelt mentioned in his 1933 inaugural speech, in fact saying that there wasn't anything to fear. One - or a nation - paralyzed by fear is, then, paralyzed, disabled by paralysis. But everyone knows what fear is, so maybe it is okay to fear fear; for a moment, perhaps. (Real fear of what we do know can, often does, cause paralysis of spirit and hope.)

But wait. Jesus healed paralytics who then walked, blind who then saw, and brought Light to illuminate Truth. He said *Fear not, for I am with you always*, too. Okay, fearing fear, then, is out, too.

How about *What! In this economy?*

Or *You can't prove that scientifically.*

The first statement is really only possible for those with much - those with little know how to continue, because it's always tough - is a statement of fearful greed made in a society willing to exchange liberty for security so they can keep their stuff, because they want more stuff, and are afraid to lose what they already have, *and* hope to get.

The second statement is typically made by people who have no concept of science, but use it to pontificate in order to justify their rejection of Truth, in order to keep doing what they want to do, to maintain their self-determined normal comfort zone.

Well, *It is what it is*, the *Fear of the unknown*, *In this economy*, and *Science* did nothing either to cause or stay the flood of water. Scientists understand and can use equations to determine how many gallons of water fell, how many cfs ran through each canyon, how many cubic yards - or metric tons - of topsoil went east, and how much raw sewage went along for the ride. And ongoing measurements of e. coli and other toxins will cause or assuage fear of contamination. And so on. (But science can't repeat the flood.)

Journalists have lots of stories to tell, and use the data scientists collect to advocate this or that position according to their bent, all without understanding, without knowledge, of any of it. They can make the story go either way, but often prey on and sow fear. But within a few weeks, when the flood is old news, and with a dramatic sigh of relief, they report that things are returning to normal, and have data and video footage to prove it. The sign under the person being interviewed says *Former Flood Victim*. All is well.

Yippee.

Being social, humans live in small and large, intimate or isolated, relationships and communities. (The internet expands their range, but that's about all.) We observe one another, compare ourselves and others to ourselves and others, and often long for something else. Even though much of what we do is done by rote - cold water, in kettle, on stove, grind beans, put grounds into press, wait for water to boil, pour over ground beans, stir water, let steep, apply and push press, pour coffee into cup, add sugar and a splash of soy, drink - God offers us many opportunities to learn character. The other day, while pouring boiling water, the lid fell off the kettle we found at the Disaster Relief Center, and the steam burned my fingers. Well, every day since, I've worn a quilted mitt to protect my fingers! (Maybe the donor decided the loose lid wasn't worth the pretty kettle and burned fingers; still it was a generous donation.)

Regardless of the donor's motivation, I'm pleased with the pretty silver kettle and the hot water to brew coffee in the little French press. We've witnessed a considerable outpouring of generosity from society in addition to that of family and friends. Every time we visit the Disaster Relief Center, cars, trucks or trailers full of items are being unloaded. Inside, they are sorted, sized, organized and then displayed by volunteers so Shan and I and others like us can shop for things we need. The only currency required is need and a FEMA registration number. Thanks, kettle donor: thanks to each generous donor! I don't mind wearing discarded clothes, cooking with used up pans or eating on donated plates with used utensils. Not at all. We had too many plates and utensils in the cabin, too much silver, too many clothes, and so on. And while we donated lots of stuff in the past, we still had too much. The flood fixed that.

But it's all just stuff, and it still appears that the loss of stuff doesn't matter to me. The other day, when a friend said it was too bad about all of my tying stuff being destroyed, I responded, "Well, I guess the stuff could have stayed dry and intact, and I could have drowned." He didn't think of that as a better solution, though. (Chuck's wife keeps telling him that when she sees or thinks of the picture of my truck drifting past, she is glad neither Shan nor I followed it, face down in the water!)

In the big, timeless picture I try to see - the one where a day is as a thousand years, and a thousand years are as a day:

the timeless picture, that is - I'm not sure what difference it makes that I wasn't washed away with the truck and the stuff; but there is purpose, and where there is life there is hope. That's because Jesus is Life, is always here; and He's timeless. For now, I'm captured in the temple that is my body, which is still fit to contain me. And the trials aren't over.

On a Friday about six weeks after the flood, between trips to the cabin, I will travel to Idaho via a flight from DIA to Spokane, Washington, where Aaron, Rachel and Addison will collect me for the 80 minute drive to their home north of Sandpoint. Shan will follow the same course, with me as chauffeur, the following Wednesday; we'll travel back to Colorado together on the next Monday. The trip, planned before the flood, is to visit our daughter, son-in-law and their first baby, who is also our first grandchild! Yay!

I started thinking that getting away would be medicinal, (I know the trip is very important for Shan, who still needs to hug Rachel and see Addison.) Instead, I got very sick with cold symptoms - while typing this a month later, I'm still sick. The flight? Rachel and Aaron had both had a cold? The letdown from flood issues? Who knows. I'm sick, don't sleep and end up not being willing to snuggle Addison Rose, aka the Bug, or Addy. She's drooling and has snot and green boogers in her nose, probably from trying to grow teeth, but who knows when it comes to babies. I don't want to infect my 6-month-old granddaughter.

Addy, aka The Bug, greets the old, tall, fat guy with a beard pull

180

(After we return to Colorado, Rachel announces that Addy also had a cold, but is well again. Babies are resilient.)

Addison is cuter than the snot that flows from her nose, and Aaron and Rachel are doing great! Addy is six-and-a-half months old, alert and responsive to everything that's going on around her. Shan spends all of her time in Addy World as she embraces - and thrives - in grandmotherhood. It fits. (Right now, Addy is sleeping, her parents are outside doing yard work, Shan is sewing something that will store or tote Addy stuff, and I'm writing.)

The baby is as excited about the tag on a pillow as she is by the flashing lights and synthetic sounds of expensive electronic toys she plays with. Peek-a-boo is popular. So is follow-daddy-with-my-eyes. The dogs, Duke and Libby, like to taste Addy - especially after she pukes delicious little flecks of goodies on her bib - and lick her hands, toes, nose, face and so on, all without an invitation. Addy doesn't seem to mind, and is doing baby very well. She is training Aaron and Rachel, and Shan and I, to be parents and grandparents, respectively. She's good at it! We're certain to be experts. The dogs are already pros at doing dog.

Today, after another nap at Rachel and Aaron's, I take a short walk to the river that flows near their home. The water is low, clear and slow. I spot several pairs and a single large trout. They're probably spawning bull trout, which, like brook trout, are actually char. I don't have polarized sunglasses yet - mine are either buried in mud in the cabin or were washed down the canyon in the flood - so fish details are not very clear. The day is sunny, and there is lots of glare on the water. But the bright, defined white on the tips of the fish's fins I can see say bull trout, which Aaron says are here. He doesn't fish the river very often: the bull trout are protected.

Before I came up, both Rachel and Aaron asked me if I wanted to go fish the Clark Fork River near Clark Fork, Idaho, with Aaron. They asked frequently; so did Shan.

(Before the flood, I probably fished 100 days a year.) During the trip that I'd planned before the flood, the idea was to go fish that area several times. But now, and every time they ask, I said no. Regardless, and in spite of the sick, I simply have no desire to go.

While I glance at and into the water, however, a short burst of how would I fish here darts through my mind, like the smaller trout I spook do through the water. But it doesn't take, is gone as soon as it appears. My shoulders slump. It leaves an empty spot where *Let's go fish* was, as though it was scoured away by rushing water. How odd. Maybe that's what happens when your trout stream is destroyed before your eyes.

I wonder. Are we presented with events that challenge our own *Why?* in a manner that goes deep enough to cut, to separate marrow and bone right where the distinguishing lines meet? (Is that a statement, observation or question?)

The sick stayed in my chest - is still there as I write this, but not as severe - and made me very tired, sore and fuzzy headed. You know. Even though I tried writing, or typing what I'd written, both were pretty much out of the question, made difficult by the fuzziness, impossible while sleeping.

I've come to think that getting sick is a part of it. It is not Life, but must be part of my body dying in the world. So far, every sick I've had has passed as my body returned to health, faster or slower depending on a variety of factors. So, when I'm sick, I've learned and decided to go with it, to sort of luxuriate in the contrast to being well, or as well as I can be at any given time. What the heck.

When chest colds attack, I cough; it hurts; I don't sleep. Often, I take Nyquil so I can sleep. And the stuff works because the combination of poisons calms the cough, and the alcohol apparently puts me out. But I have odd dreams when I take it.

For the most part, I really don't need any help to have odd, vivid dreams. Maybe my vivid awake imagination carries over to asleep visions, in order to play out or finish the path I trod while awake. Who knows? Again, I go with it rather than fighting it. Like other musings, one must wade through the garbage and sort out what matters, to determine which may have purpose.

But the Nyquil-induced sleep, on top of an already fatigued and now sick mind, delivered nightmares that were dark but not black, were wet but not fluid. They were, in fact, gooey, mucky, brown, and persistent.

Three of my favorite five girls
Shan, Addy, Rachel

And the dreams, which ran as on a loop, over and over and over, made me feel nauseous. Sometimes, I woke for a moment and tried to cast them out by thinking of something else. Well, I'm here to report that being surrounded by nauseating brown mucky goo is hard to replace during a sick, drug-induced sleep. I tried. But too soon, my thoughts of wading in a trout stream, hearing - and smelling - the crystal clear flow of water, were overtaken by the compelling visage and scent of mucky brown goo. Yuk!

So I went with it instead of fighting it. I mean I was already very sick, felt awful, was tired and dreary: what's a little gooey brown muck going to do? Right? Wrong! I started to feel very isolated and empty, which had to do with the oppressive nature of the nightmare. Because, as I went with it, the dream got worse with each repetition. My imagination revealed more details as the nightmare expanded and developed its theme.

183

Of course the mucky brown goo was flood residue that covered, coated or settled around everything that Shan and I had lived with for a long time. While those things weren't our life, probably weren't even normal, they were there with us, and in the dream, their individual charm evoked memories of events, people, and doing things together. Soiled pictures are easy to put in their place, and if you knew how much Shan and I enjoyed watching DVD's together, for example, you'd understand how seeing them covered in the goo fit, too. Shan's sewing and my tying stuff were individual hobbies that we both encouraged one another to pursue, and knowing Addy slept under a quilt Shan designed and sewed, or recalling a trip to the stream with Russ where we'd cast flies I'd tied, or tying flies with Aaron; well, you get it.

For, you see, the detail of the nightmare had me sitting in the gooey brown muck, surrounded by its stench, while reaching into and retrieving one item that evoked memories, people, an event, and then trying to clean away the brown gooey muck while someone offered me a brown mucky goo covered snack to eat. Like I said, it was nauseating. It was demeaning. It was awful.

To increase the dream's charm, the mucky gooey brown wouldn't come off. After every wipe of the always filthy cloth, which initially spread and sometimes thinned the yuk on the memory being cleaned - and the snack being offered - the brown mucky goo reappeared, mucked up everything, including the person that went with it. Thus, the emptiness, the sense of isolation. (Snack handlers, whose voices I heard, were never visible in the nightmare, other than the brown mucky goo gloved hand that held the offered snack.)

Well, this went on for several days, staying the same in vision while becoming less shocking to, but more repulsive in, my emotions. The repetition piled up; my compromised position, weakened by illness, worsened, all a part of the sick in its own luxuriant way. (A little like feeling great and eating too much Turkish Delight, perhaps.) And by luxuriating in this excess of yuk, I became inordinately self-possessed, which was very uncomfortable. For awhile, this empty me-ness convinced me that I'd lost the story, too.

And then I felt empty, indeed.

I've come to think, probably because I know, that in weakness God makes me strong by invading the emptiness, which indicates need, with Holy Spirit, Who is Jesus. Call it all Love. And I also think, and maybe, too, because I know, this opening, if you please, is also an invitation by and to Satan to send one of his devils, also bright light, to trick me into becoming a fool; to believe lies. Well, it was Jesus who invaded my emptiness, who replaced the visage of brown mucky goo with Light and Truth.

Truth and Time go hand in hand, and Jesus Is Truth thoughts mean I now know - the lesson again taught during the brown mucky goo episode - that His Light is brightest because He Is. Time dispels and Truth casts out the lies of Satan's bright, but dull-by-comparison, dim glimmer.

During an illness, which is separation from health, there is a yearning to be tempted into selfish helplessness, to know emptiness and to feel, in such tyranny, that it is permanent, that it will last forever. In reality, we know that we don't know what the next moment will bring; we know it's brought death to many, and we know that one day it will be, in the flesh, our lot to share.

Satan wants us to feel separated from God, dead to Life. He wants us to believe lies, to stay dead, to live as though we're dead while thinking we're living. Even as we try to wipe away the brown mucky goo so we can see - because we do try: it's God calling us to trust and obey while He offers Living water - Satan provides more brown gooey muck because he has it to give, and nothing more, in abundance.

God is Life, and wants us to be complete: alive. Why is this such a difficult choice?

LOSS AND PERSPECTIVE

One thing about losing stuff is knowing that I don't resent having given things away in the past. Stuff in use is better than things lost in mud, or washed away by water, or burned by fire, or eaten by moths.

My unofficially adopted son, Keith, was at the cabin while Jeff and Geert visited those few days before the flood. He fished, watched the tying - he's an excellent fly tier, but was happy to observe and drink cold beer - and gave me grief, as any good son will. When Keith visits, he likes to go through and fondle dry fly capes and saddles that I've collected over the past 22 years. Often, he hides one in his stuff, but then - at least I think! - he always lets me see it so we both know he's teasing; I've given him a lot of feathers, but the kid always wants more. (Shan hides the candy.)

On Monday before the flood, Jeff had to get to DIA for his flight back to Texas, and Keith had to go back to southwest Denver to work. Keith agreed to deliver Jeff to the airport, and after we fished the morning away - it started raining hard before we finished, and didn't stop until after the flood - Keith and Jeff packed their bags while I made them each a sandwich. When Keith sat his bag on the living room floor, saddle feathers poked out in every direction: he'd put all of my dry fly tying saddles into the bag, and had a big, feather eating grin on his face. We played a big fight over the theft, he negotiated to give a few back, but then relented when he returned all of them before he and Jeff said their good-byes to Geert and I.

And a few days later, I wished he had taken all of the pelts. (He probably does, too!)

At seven weeks and two days off the mountain, certain images are dimmer, the edges of emotions less cutting. But time always does its work, dulling edges while sharpening perspective. And getting perspective has merit.

I felt happy for Shan when she returned to work. Friends, patients, the office and comfortable routines allowed part of her mind to settle into a familiar pace for four days each week. Each workday begins with her morning ablutions, beautification - she doesn't need the help - breakfast and the scurry to get out of the house and to the office. Each day's challenges follow, but for the first month or so, Shan has generous, kind support from the rest of the office staff. (This continues to be the case.) Certain pettiness that recently bared its ugly fangs washed away, and other than doing the great work everyone in this office always does, the focus was on supporting Shan. It was delightful, a salve for Shan's raw nerves and jumpy emotions. Within a few moments of clocking out and starting the car for her drive back to the farm, Shan calls to tell me she is on her way, and reports about the day. She includes happy anecdotes about the team, patients, the doctor, and tales of people she met who also had flood-related stories. A dentist from Lyons, who could not get to his office, was going to work in Shan's office; kids from Lyons were going to Longmont schools; parents' businesses were destroyed, homes damaged, and so on. Shan listens, encourages, and then relates the meaningful events to me.

I'm always glad when she hasn't had many entity calls, and try to spare her the frustration and impatience I suffer almost every day: I filter the lousy out and only relay details that matter. For the first couple weeks, we ate out, went to the Disaster Relief Center, visited Jessica at the Coffee Tree, or went shopping for stuff we needed to make it through each day. (There are things we take for granted!) It's interesting how little things we use each day are missed when they've been ruined by, or remain in, floodwater or mud. Buying more stuff meant figuring out where to store more stuff in the small farm house, which meant buying stuff to store stuff. We made a few mistakes along the way, returned items to the Disaster Relief Center or donated them to an ARC Thrift Store, and tried not to buy stuff if we were at all confused. It is better to wait and make good decisions than to provide more fodder for dumps.

Each evening, if I'd missed going during the day, Shan and I went to the Post Office to check our box. For the first few weeks, we found cards with notes of encouragement and prayers; checks, gift cards or cash were often enclosed. Boxes of thoughtful gifts arrived with socks, clothing, knickknacks, devotionals, and so on. Shan cried as she read the cards, or saw who had written to us. We were, and are, humbled by the outpouring of generosity that people expressed.

On these common grounds, Shan and I rejoiced and found ourselves thankful. In our own relations, we often struggled. Shan thought I was mean when I tried to look objectively at and deal with daily issues, and she often responded with what I felt was rudeness towards me. She was quick to be defensive when I confronted what I thought were her irrational comments or emotions; or when I asked about her ongoing forgetfulness and lack of focus. In other words, we both responded out of the emotions we experienced while disregarding our mate's feelings, without perspective about what they saw and thought about each day's events, which added to the flood experience and how we were dealing with it. But the commitment we'd made to one another by the strength of our wills and within the purview of God's grace - our deepening love for each other - overcame all of our selfish pettiness as we dealt with each event, with the problems each day brought or solved. I'm not convinced we've conquered anything, and as I write that word I am convinced it's not an actual fight, anyway. But we're on track to gain character and patience as we persevere through all things, through these curious circumstances. And we know it's not our power that does it, but the strength of God's might, of His gift of faith, knowing that He will complete that which He began, that the flood and its aftermath are all enclosed within His will. It rains on those who love Him, on those who don't.

As the days turned into weeks, and now at the past-two-months' mark, Shan seems to have sorted through a lot, has come to grips with what to hold onto and what to let go of. She has courage, which is character on display. The new hot buttons both of us know the other has - it's funny how we can identify them in someone else without acknowledging them in ourselves - are now pushed less often, and even when pushed, have cooled. Maybe it's because some of the heat is off - the water's down - or because we now accept the veracity of time, the efficacy of the work it has done, know it will continue doing.

In fact, though, Shan has become more emotionally stable as I've slipped a bit. I'm certain some of it is fatigue - I've slept fitfully or very little, taken few naps - but some of it is an ongoing battle based on what I believe. This has much to do with my inquisitiveness and the examination of what is true, which continues until I recall that the issue is knowing Who Is Truth. I'm often confused by the materialistic train of thinking that has been imbedded into my system by the world without, even though I know, I believe, Jesus has replaced the death I often sense in my members with Life: His Life. Of course I see dimly and in a mirror, rather than face to face, but long to know as I am now known: this is a battle of the mind for control of my will, of my thoughts and emotions. The question isn't *What shall I do*, but *Whom shall I believe, Whom shall I obey?* His yoke is light: *I believe, Lord; help me in my unbelief.*

189

That prayer always results in new challenges that are met with either contempt and disdain, or with hope and by faith. When met by the latter pair, patience, character and a renewed mind emerge, like a butterfly escaping its chrysalis. By faith, I am mounted on eagle's wings and take flight, soaring and luxuriating in the reality of God's love and grace. By faith, I'm at liberty to be of the I Am.

Through it all, I am aware of being thankful, aware of joy even when things feel awful and smell bad. I'm also aware of further challenges living in the world, and of God's gift of faith that keeps me from the world; even though the barbs hurt, the flesh continues to die and decay.

A wild, beautiful Big Thompson River rainbow trout barbless dry fly in jaw

THE RIVER

One of the issues being discussed post-flood is what to do with the river. A stream coalition has been formed and people have attended meetings where experts and others discuss the river issue. From what I see, the primary purpose of the discussions, and the hope for those involved, is to determine how to move, manipulate and control the river so property will not be damaged in the future when the already manipulated and channelized stream has the opportunity, as it did during the flood, to actually be a river. Right now, with all of the leftover drama from the flood, with the cost of road and other reconstruction, damage and so on constantly flashed before people's eyes and blared into their ears, I wouldn't be surprised if the government suggested, and the governed agreed, to dig the river to a constant 20 feet deep, 40-feet wide, and put chain link fences around it to keep people safe, as is done near playgrounds and bike paths built by irrigation ditches. After all, a river is simply a natural irrigation ditch that must be fixed in order to carry water that serves homes, people, industry and agriculture.

But in the past week (I write this edit in early January 2014) my opinion has changed. While I still think many government entities would prefer what they see as the easiest way out - dig that channel to protect the road, to carry water safely out of the foothills and onto the thirsty plains - in fact, there are numerous people and entities, even within government agencies, who are committed to repairing and restoring the river so it has natural, stable banks that will host healthy riparian habitat. As it turns out, doing so, which will support trout because what they need is clean, cold, oxygenated water, is less expensive and faster to build than traditional concrete diversions and channelized structures that also, as it turns out, enhance flood damage and destruction. Of course the votes are out, but the prognosis is encouraging; there is hope that the Big Thompson will once again be a great trout stream, and will be safe and stable during adverse conditions, too.

The Big Thompson River is a dandy trout stream that teems with life. Trout, the aquatic insects they eat, and many other organisms and wildlife, thrive in and around the stream's clean, cold water: they require a healthy river to do so. It happens to flow through a narrow, steep, awesome canyon that has also been developed to accommodate hundreds of homes, businesses, and parks. To get there, the road was built and vehicles drive millions of miles on it each year. Because travel and commerce are the number one priority and use, the river that made the canyon - and is the top attraction in the canyon - has been rerouted and manipulated out of expediency and convenience, putting it at the bottom of the totem pole unless it misbehaves.

The flood began with heavy, persistent rain that soaked the ground and filled thousands of acres of sandy soil with water. And it continued because the falling water had nowhere else to go. Once saturated, water slid over the soil's sodden surface, pulled by gravity ever lower along the path of least resistance.

As well-defined paths filled, they overflowed and the water cut new transits until small but growing rivulets dumped water into larger rivulets that eventually joined once dry gulches, before emptying into the stream.

Water created rivulets and raced off the mountainside, added to the very high water in the river, then went where it wanted, filling our canyon from wall to wall

The flood became a flood when the trout stream's bed could no longer contain the wealth of water. Not greedy, the river let it go and the water did as it had done in the miniature at higher elevations but now on a larger scale. The river cut new courses, filled low areas, and continued to flow through the canyon to lower elevations. At our place in Drake, after leaving its prescribed course, the original 40-foot-wide riverbed was soon filled with rocks, rubble, gravel, sand and other debris. The water, from one foot to more than a dozen feet deep, filled the width of our canyon, over two hundred yards across, from one side to another. And it roared, taking whatever it pleased with its powerful flow. I guess the gravity bill was paid in full. It certainly pulled surplus water out of our canyon and onto the plains.

While our flood was fast and furious, a speck on history's long time line, it's easy to feel as though the damage is permanent. During, and then in its aftermath, the river has been made the demon of our flood, in part because it is the course the water followed, along which the damage was done. I don't think anything or anyone could have stayed the water by their own act of personal power. It rained hard and for a long time: the water had to go somewhere. But it appears that less damage might have been wrought with foresight rather than expediency.

As the river, obedient to gravity, replaced the contrived, circumstantial, and convenient, so does one obedient to God become free from sin. This obedient one is made alive. All things are for this one's freedom and God's glory.

The main post-flood/rescue focus was *fix the roads.* Makes sense, of course, because without roads through the canyons little access is available to homes, businesses and mountain towns. As mentioned, the effort and execution to repair and rebuild the road in our canyon was Herculean and Hermesian: strong and fast! In order to accomplish it, though, the river bed, which had a full opportunity to express where it wanted to go, was moved for the convenience of the road work.

Following the '76 flood, which did significant road damage, Colorado road engineers designed and rebuilt the road to supposedly withstand a 500-year flood event. At least that's what I heard, and what was repeated following our flood as Colorado's governor and CDOT road experts discussed the how and how much concerning this rebuilding session. The governor at one time asked something about how much money should be spent in light of the possibility that we'd be back here within 20 to 40 years after a future flood. I thought it was a good question. But there are other good questions that aren't being asked.

Over the past few months I've attended a few river restoration meetings, and read web pages and news articles concerning what to do with the river. And a few bright, thoughtful hydrologists - people who study and work with water and streams - have discussed the damage water does or can do, comparing wild river courses with those manipulated by man. The consensus is that contrived channelization of a streambed is neither safe nor effective in moving large amounts of flowing water because the forces of the water destroy channelized configurations by undermining and destroying the armored banks - banks lined with large boulders - before the river goes where it wants while creating a natural shape and definition. While going where it wants, it also destroys other things in its way, like roads, bridges, structures and landscapes.

This, in other words, is precisely what happened in 1976 and again in 2013. I will tell you that I knew the river well, and paid attention to its banks, vegetation, structure and so on while I waded and fished in it. And the stretches of the Big T Canyon that incurred the most significant road and property damage were the stretches that had been channelized and maintained as such since the 1976 flood. It was in these areas that the channel was manipulated, straightened and armored, then the road elevated and built parallel to it from a few to dozens of feet from the river, with the idea that the channel would safely move the water downstream, that the road and other property would be safe. It didn't work.

And now, in the scurry of excellent road work, the same thing has been done again. In areas where the stream moved - and where there is room and it could have stayed where it went, where hydrologists hired by CDOT to make recommendations said it should remain - the river was put back in its old bed. In most cases, the 1976 manipulated bed filled with stones, rocks and sand during our flood, but CDOT - the controllers of this work - dug out the old bed, usually digging it deeper and with steeper banks, in order to use existing bridges or out of convenience. (In our neighborhood, for example, CDOT hired, then ignored a hydrologist's advise to leave the new riverbed where it was in order to use a $100,000 bridge. They rebuilt that channelized streambed in the same spot that had just contributed to many millions of dollars in road and property damage. What has been done in order to use that bridge assures similar damage in the next flood. I suppose the bridge will survive again, though, so there is that savings to consider.)

So far, when confronted with this observation, those directing the work say the work on the river is temporary, is being done so the road and property will be safe during 2014 runoff. And people interested in restoring and making the river better seem to be buying that line. But I don't believe it. When does the government purposely spend millions of dollars to do temporary things? All of the armoring being done looks permanent to me.

I think the same lack of vision following the 1976 Flood has been repeated during the months following the 2013 Flood. Perhaps the people who made decisions in 1976 lacked the experience and knowledge to make correct determinations and decisions; but the similarities of damage done in this flood, in part as a result of decisions, designs and repairs done following the '76 flood, and the lack of adjustments in the work that's followed this flood are beyond comprehension.

Didn't a wise person say something to the effect that a fool does the same thing the same way and hopes for different results? Another about those who fail to learn from history are destined to repeat it? Well, it's being played out right now, right before our eyes.

What about the trout and wildlife? We saw herds of Bighorn Sheep along the temporary road on both of our early trips back to the canyon. Based on past observations - and the fact that a similar destructive event struck this canyon a mere 37 years before - we know that nature is resilient. Animals know how to survive. Insect life returns fast, as do certain types of vegetation. Homeowners are being encouraged to buy and sow particular grass seeds in order to keep noxious weeds from growing. I suspect the state and county will do the same. Replacing trees will take longer.

In early December, my friend, the writer Dennis Smith, sent me a link to an article about a Big Thompson Canyon post-flood trout survey done by a Colorado fisheries' biologist. The data was taken in November 2013 when access to the canyon was available. The data report that from Olympus Dam downstream to the Waltonia Bridge - the ten miles that are designated as catch and release water (anglers can only use flies or artificial lures and must revive and release all trout) - thirty percent more trout are in the stream than before the flood. (The stretch also had much less road and riverbed damage because there had been much less channelization after 1976. This time, water left the natural bed, but returned to it as the flood water receded.) The biologist suggests this is due to fish that were washed out of Lake Estes during high flows. There is no data on aquatic insects. He also reports that near Drake, and at several other collection sites farther down the canyon, only 5 to 20 percent of the earlier trout population remained.

The data is encouraging; the trout are still there. I'm quite certain that the insects will repopulate the stream, probably starting with midges and caddis: both types are hearty and vigorous. I'm also sure that willows, grasses and other vegetation will grow as long as people leave the stream's banks alone. I wonder about summer water temperatures; worry they'll become elevated due to the lack of vegetation; wonder how much water will move down the stream, and so on. I suspect the river needs a good, healthy flushing flow that 2014 runoff should provide if they'll let the water flow down the river instead of through pipes. But overall, I'm pleased with what I read, hopeful that the river will soon return to good health.

The Big Thompson River Restoration Coalition (BTRRC - find it on the web) is working to identify river stakeholders. The group consists of federal, state and county government entities, businesses, homeowners, anglers and other interested parties. It's a diverse group with various ideas and goals that are often at odds with one another. Building a consensus - the group wants to restore the Big Thompson River so it is safe, healthy and beautiful - is going to be tough duty. I've asked if they have identified the people who actually make the decisions - most of the panels consist of workers who are following directives from above - and if they know how to convince decision makers to do the right thing. So far the answers are not clear, are accompanied by *We need to put our best foot forward.* Fair enough! I hope it works. So far, as mentioned earlier, what I see is work done out of expediency and convenience that will be neither safe nor beautiful, and will be expensive to make safe and beautiful. I guess we'll see.

Looking east from the farm, the sun rises yet again!

THIS STORY

This story, then, is one of hope. Ongoing hope that is not disappointed regardless of destructive circumstances, loss, rudeness, confusion and disjointedness. Because hope does not disappoint. His appointment is found in hope, and with ears that hear - an exercise of the will that refuses to listen to either the cacophony of contrarian noise or to soothing lies. I know, trust, and believe that in Christ all things were made and have their being, that all things are sustained, that in Him all things find fullness and are made complete. That's where hope abides: in Him. Through it all, He is making me completely human, full of Life and fully aware of being in Christ: Creator, Sustainer and Future of all things.

"All things were made by him, and without him was not anything made that was made. In him was life (eternal); and the life was the light of men. And the light shined in darkness; and the darkness comprehended it not." John 1:3-5.

"When I was a child, I spoke as a child, I understood as a child: but when I became a man, I put away childish things. For now we see through a glass [in a mirror], darkly; but then face to face: now I know in part; but then shall I know even as also I am known. And now abides faith, hope, love, these three; but the greatest of these is love." I Corinthians 13: 11-13.

"And this is condemnation, that light is come into the world, and men loved darkness rather than light, because their deeds were evil. For every one that doeth evil hateth the light, neither comes to the light, lest his deeds should be reproved. But he that does truth cometh to the light, that his deeds may be made manifest, that they were wrought in God." John 3: 19-21.

One whose mind is renewed by God's regeneration of new birth - born of the Spirit - first comes to the Light. And the all dark consuming brightness exposes habits, thoughts, and a developed, often entrenched, style that worked evil, out of the flesh and of the world, through that one's history. Thus, continued renewal is required, and proves God's good, perfect and acceptable will for the one now being renewed.

Those who continue to love darkness hate the Light. Because their deeds are evil, they stay there - in darkness - by an act of their will, eyes closed so they won't know the Light. Meanwhile, the one who lives Truth comes to the Light and that one, and others who open their eyes, know all good deeds are wrought in God. He does the work that is freedom for one in the Light.

Have you ever seen a field of Kansas sunflowers as their happy yellow faces turn to and follow the light of the sun all throughout the day? A plant seeking, finding, and loving light. Of course having no independent will - God graced sunflowers with beauty and tasty seeds - plants do as they are made, and do plant very well.

I want to do human as fully, to be completely human. And my will, when it turns away from Light, chooses poorly.

Every event offers the opportunity to choose to be in, then act either in or apart from Light: I can do truth in the Light, and know that deed is wrought in God. And while my history and past definitely are populated by habits, thoughts and a style musty with darkness, the next choice might be done by faith. *I long to do truth, Lord; will I?*

It's not a can or can't argument, so much as a will or won't choice. What will I choose? Whom will I follow by faith and in obedience? Will I open my eyes and see Light? Allow the searing heat of His Light to cleanse, to dispel darkness?

Water, which we add soap to in order to clean, in the case of the flood left a muddy, yucky mess.

For the most part, it appears that I don't treasure the stuff that I've accumulated, used, given away, and so on. It's the only reason I can see that makes, or allows me to answer the question, *Why don't you mourn the loss of your stuff?* with *I just don't.* It's probably why the slight blip of enthusiasm I had at the thought of salvaging items was only slight, and that the work of cleaning, disinfecting and so on, has been so onerous to me. The flood, muck, rot, and sewage odors nauseate me. I feel filthy after cleaning items. And when I'm forced to discard stuff that we put time and energy into salvaging, then cleaning, the waste, the sense of loss, increases.

I wonder how I'll feel about tying flies with what were mud-caked, sewage-water infused feathers? Who knows.

Yes, there are items I still hope to salvage and then use, so maybe I'll feel different after the cleaning work is complete. For the most part, though, it seems that none of it is all that important.

When I try to explain this to inquiring friends or acquaintances, they, who have all of their stuff, easily say, *Well, it's only stuff,* and I sometimes think, *Yeah, but not your stuff,* when their tone and manner say, *I'm sure glad it wasn't my stuff.* It's pretty easy to look from afar. I know because I've done that.

I've always been able to identify and commiserate with fellow sufferers of back or other chronic pain because I've had it for so long. And after my dad died, I had a new and deeper appreciation for familial loss. The flood is bringing new perspective, too. How will Father use it to encourage others, to make us free? I guess we'll see.

Through the ups and downs of dealing with various emotions and thoughts of my own, of Shan's, and of those imposed on us by both thoughtful and thoughtless others, I continue to know His Light is here right now, throughout, and always. His Grace and Love continue and abide, apparently because He grafted me into the vine of Life: it's His doing, and I agree to it. And He provides succor throughout. *Abide in Me as I abide in My Father; make us one, Father God, as We are One. I in Thee and they in Me.* Jesus said something like that; look it up.

It's true.

A weed may mime the vine, but it will be cut off and cast into God's consuming fire. The Christian doesn't mimic Jesus, but by faith Christ lives in the Christian, which is the how and the why of being one. Jesus made it so.

Christianity is not some sort of romantic fantasy full of concocted lists of rules and regulations that has a happy ending. That is Christendom, an institutionalized habit that becomes its own bureaucratic cesspool of stinky muck. The light reveals this, even though groups of individuals who love darkness rather than light, make up congregations of self-important pontificating fools.

And yet, little things have meant, and continue to mean, a lot to Shan and me. You know, basic creature comforts, conveniences we've come to expect, often to feel we deserve, because we live in the richest, freest country in the history of humanity. We're free to consume, to waste, to covet, to use minerals and energy carelessly. We've earned it.

Before we waded out of the cabin on Thursday, water rising day, I looked at a picture frame we'd put on the counter, then snatched and put it in the bag I had. And I sort of forgot about it until later that night. Our hostess, and Ed and Sarah, had retired to the two bedrooms, and Shan and I were left in the living room. We had a flashlight. There were two couches, one short, the other long. We'd brought our pillows and a couple fleece blankets that we'd missed for water absorption. The rain fell. The river rumbled with water and rolling boulders. It was dark.

After we said good night, took to our respective couch and tried to get comfortable, longing for sleep, I remembered the picture frame, took it out of the bag and shined a flashlight beam on it. "Look," I said.

Shan did. And we both stated to giggle. Then, Shan cried.

The frame, you see, holds three expressive photos of Addison Rose that were taken in July 2013 while she and her parents sat on the deck at the cabin. Each is a gem, but together they say that new life - including baby girl life - is great! Now, when we look at the photos, Shan and I remember that moment and still share a giggle that has deep meaning. Life is good.

When we moved onto the farm, we were told, and believed, that we were welcome to stay. The lack of a kitchen, but the availability of a roof, heat, power, hot water, a bathroom and a bed, seemed a fair exchange for a bit of stability. And a week later, when the owners told us that we were welcome to stay through the end of November - which seemed far away (it was yesterday) - rent free, that beginning on December 1 we'd be charged a fair rental price, and could stay as long as we liked, we knew we had a place to stay, where we'd have space and time to let answers and decisions important but still out of our purview work their way out, and we could figure out how we'd respond, what we could do. Cool beans, eh?

And when the family decided to put in a kitchen, which meant a fridge, gas stove and sink, we had a rush of gratitude accompanied by a further sigh of relief. After all, eating out and washing cereal bowls in the tiny bathroom sink started getting old for us, aging in dog years as we felt at the time.

It was the sink that made Shan cry, though. I think the shock of convenience caused the tears, because rinsing stuff off in a kitchen sink, simple and commonplace as it is, turns out to be a not-to-be-taken-for-granted privilege after all. Kind of like breaking a few fingers on the hand you wipe your butt with. I mean the gas range and refrigerator are great, but everything but the kitchen sink does not, as it turns out, a kitchen make.

We're doing fine without a disposal, without a dishwasher, and so on. I think we're less complacent about dirty dishes, so we clean them just after they are used, or just before the next use. (We don't have many dishes now.) And the little kitchen, made brighter, more full of light by the small window that the family installed above the kitchen sink (!) is all we need, and more, as it turns out, than we deserve.

Looking out the little kitchen window, which faces east, in the morning is a new delight for us. We can see the horizon, can see the sun actually rise for a change. Living in Drake at 6,200 feet in elevation, we were surrounded by 8,000+ foot high mountains, a part of the foothills that support the Continental Divide to the west. There, we had filtered sun light that, depending on the season, only became direct when the sun rose high enough and at the right angle that its rays cleared the foothills, then touched and entered the cabin. All of the trees on the property blocked it, too. (That won't be a problem if we rebuild.) During winter, we had less than five hours of direct light, which was tough for me. In fact, it was a bit morbid.

Here, I think, the extra sunlight has been a blessing, has been medicinal. In fact, even though I'm still not sleeping well, I'm also taking fewer naps. There really is something fine about sunlight, about Light, and light, that exposes lies and truth, and illuminates. It's cheery. And Colorado's front range boasts 300-plus days of sunshine a year.

The kitchen sink, and the sunshine, are simple blessings which I do not take for granted but which I am thankful for.

Thanks!

Ah, the little things. As soon as we were off the mountain, Russ and Brittany went shopping and bought Shan and me a variety of necessities, and immediately shipped them to Jess' Loveland apartment. The box was stuffed with socks, undies, T-shirts, a sweater for me, various clothing items for Shan, and a little treat. Russ told me in his matter-of-fact way, "I'm sending Moleskines." It was one of the few statements, or things, that made me want to cry.

Russ knew I'd want to write; he knew the simple comfort of writing in a thin Moleskines lined journal. The set of 3 jumped out of the box, and, after caressing the smooth cover, I immediately started to jot thoughts, write notes, record stories and memories of the flood. It was therapeutic and more, as Russ knew it would be, because he's a writer, too.

When the first set of 3 Moleskine lined journals were nearly filled, I called and asked Russ where I could find more. "Target," he said. I went early the next morning and bought 6, two sets of 3, and a small Moleskine ruled notebook, which I like to carry with me at all times, just in case. While I'm into the second set of three journals, I haven't cracked the notebook, instead using a little spiral, cardboard bound piece of junk and filling it with odoriferous notes from bureaucratic and insurance entities. I guess I have enough polluted stuff, so I'll wait to use the classy notebook for meaningful scribbles. The other one I had, and all of its notes, was ruined in the flood. I saw it on the bedroom floor, soaked with water and caked in mud, and didn't even pick it up, let alone open it.

And that, like the loss of other journals, writings and my compositions, created over a period of more than 40 years, did make me a little sad.

Ah, but the wonder - the hope! - of a fresh Moleskine. And how different they feel when crumpled full of words! Great! For me, better than the kitchen sink, I think.

But not better than the Light.